The Secret Life Of Teenagers

Calvin White

The Key Publishing House Inc.

This is a non-fiction work based on the experience of the book's author Calvin White. Names and places of students mentioned have been disguised where appropriate for privacy. Whenever actual characters are mentioned, permission has been granted for inclusion in this book. All artwork included in this book is obtained by permission from its owners

First Edition 2013
The Key Publishing House Inc.
Toronto, Canada
Website: www.thekeypublish.com
E-mail: info@thekeypublish.com

ISBN 978-1-926780-42-9
eISBN 978-1-926780-53-5

Copyediting by Vickie Ferguson
Cover design and typesetting by Narinder Singh

Printed and bound in USA.

Published by a grant and in association with The Key Research Center (www.thekeyresearch.org). The Key promotes freedom of thought and expression and peaceful coexistence among human societies.

KPH
The Key Publishing House Inc.
www.thekeypublish.com
www.thekeyresearch.org

For all those kids who opened up to their truth and included me on the journey and for my five children and Jacquie, all of whom too often came second.

Acknowledgements

With gratitude and thanks to my counsellor colleagues: John Collingridge, Linda Grey, Debbie Almquist, and Lynda Tedesco who inspired me and shared the path. Also thanks to my principals: Nick Watkins, Greg Kitchen, Glenn Borthistle, and Joe Rhodes for their toleration and support — and to my many vice-principals. To all my teacher colleagues: those still at it - find ways to make it fun; those who have moved on - thanks for the memories.

Thanks to Mike Donaldson for his insight, advice, and editing.

Special appreciation goes to the students whose artifact writing and art-work appears in this book, some of whom are not identified in order to protect their privacy. Similarly, none of the case studies feature the real names of the students they depict.

Specific thanks:
Cover art: Katie Crane, Grade 12
Art on Page 57: Stacey Malysh
Art on Page 98: Chris Korytko
Art on Page 127: Kayla Fulton

I am in ~~teeth~~ ~~green~~ living with my real dad ~~another~~ it was a fun time when I was there because all the things my dad did I thought were right but when I got back to ~~Amara~~ I realized that some things he did with me wernt ~~so~~ right and some of those things were feeling my balls and penis up and in the mournings he used ~~to~~ to feel or touch my penis when it was erect because I needed a ~~p~~ piss or other times in the shower the would wash my back and grab my bum and squeeze it like men do to women another time he masterbated me in the bath tub ~~xxxxxxxxxxx~~ and he said he was checking to can if my dink was in working order and all the time he would say I was the one who ~~bore~~ you took you from your moms stomach ~~so~~ dont be embarest to show me your ~~penis put~~ ~~other~~ times he would ask me about my experiences with girls and make me or force it out of me to tell him in great detail what I did and they did to ~~me~~ and I didnt like it ~~xxxxx~~ ~~xxxxxxxxxx~~   JAMES - 15 YEARS OLD

Contents

Today I drove for the first time and thankfully it was a great experience and accident free. Now I really wish I had taken my drivers test on time. Before this I could never see myself in the drivers seat

Seth – 16 years old

Introduction

Who gets called a lazy piece of shit? Who gets fondled by their best friend's dad? Who lies under the covers while a man with a gun walks into the bedroom? The children in our schools, of course. I'm not talking about the fringe kids or the inner city; I'm talking middle class and mainstream. And these are the memories and experiences our teenagers carry while moving from class to class in the high schools of our country.

For thirty years, I've listened to the truths of our kids. Within the security of my office walls, they release their stories, usually with hesitation and fear, sometimes with tears. Then they walk back out into the hallways, their public face on, to the world they feel more control over, the reality that is predictable and orderly.

In their classes, they are simply those faces, nothing more. They are instructed, given assignments, and graded on their performance. Teachers think of them as A, B, or C students. Or as failures. Teachers react at any bad behaviour and expect disciplinary consequences from the administration. "Seat warmers" are those who come to class but don't engage sufficiently or don't hand in work. Absenteeism is condemned. Phone calls are made to homes, enquiring why so and so has been missing school. Parent meetings are arranged in which teachers and/or administrators relay the negative information to the parents and discuss how to get a better performance from the kid. Everything would appear as though it's straightforward. Everything would appear as though the kid's best interests are in the minds of all.

Meanwhile, the father is an alcoholic or workaholic, the mom is secretly seeing someone else, the step-dad calls his step-daughter a fat bitch, and the kid herself is clinically depressed. No one talks about that. The teenager will not publicly betray the parents, and isn't brave or self-aware enough to clearly speak about his inner self.

In my office, one of the key components of my counselling relationship has always been secrecy. If the teenager thinks I'll tell their secrets, why on earth would they open up? So, I promise it is all confidential. In fact, I go out of my way to explain that once we both leave the office and I see the kid in the hallways or a classroom that I don't see them as the person who was just then in my office, revealing all their truths but as a student going about their business. I want them to feel secure, want them to know they don't have to wonder what I'm thinking or seeing.

Being a teenager has never been so difficult. Yet, I don't know how many times I've heard adults claim they know all about it because they, too, were teenagers once. Well, in actual fact, they don't know. Their memories are fading. Their reality was different. There was no computer, no cell phone, no text messaging, no super potent marijuana, no crystal meth, no pornography downloaded on cell phones, no video games, no overflow of money and leisure, no free long distance telephone calls. They weren't so inundated with information, so much so that it's all but impossible to discern which is relevant or even true. They didn't graduate with so many options that it is basically a fluke that any kid can ever know which direction to go. They didn't grow up with the same level or nature of stress.

Teenagers, by definition, have always been the true in-betweeners. They are absolutely emotionally undeveloped and still in need of much nurturing and guidance, yet they have a growing awareness, a growing power, that allows them to see the flaws around them and to take action as a response. They can now fight, drink, take drugs, say no, rebel, run away, and buy things. They are powerless to change situations in their homes for the better, but they no longer have to suffer blindly and can behave in ways that relieve some of the stress.

The teenage stage has been dismissed as being filled with angst, as though the angst is somehow not legitimate, not founded in reality. This angst is more accurately understood as worry, as being in the time of firsts. The first time to feel awareness of one's parents' shortcomings. The first time to know existential loneliness and vulnerability. The first time to feel a full spectrum of love and intimacy for a peer. The first time of being aware of feeling uncertain, of feeling rejectable, of feeling the intense need to belong, to be good enough. The first time of feeling the full brunt of losing a boyfriend or girlfriend, of being cheated on, of having to deal with a roving eye of one's own. The first time of being bludgeoned with the notion they must be responsible and mature.

The first time of truly understanding that they are supposed to become somebody worthy.

It has always been a terrible stage to be in. But now it has all speeded up. The cushions, the sheltering, the restraints have all been shucked. There are no protections anymore. Teenagers, and now those far younger, are all fair game for all who want to make a buck. Drug dealer, porn purveyor, clothes manufacturer, toymaker - they all go after teens with a vengeance. The adult world has subsumed everything. Anything goes and our kids have to make it through the minefield with very little meaningful or knowledgeable support. Nike's old slogan was "Just Do It!" That's become the dictum, as shallow and stupid as it is, which is applied to our kids. Get out there and perform. Don't do anything wrong, and don't succumb to any of the baser temptations.

Every graduation exercise in the country trots out the same flat and phony creed. "This is your time. Go make your way in the world and create your success." The creed is really for all the adults. The ruse is necessary to protect us from our own shame and our own sense of failure and helplessness, our own willful blindness.

When a teen comes into my office and opens up, it feels like I'm breathing oxygen. Their insight, their authenticity, their courage inspires. I leave some sessions believing the planet is in better shape than I had thought because our kids are so beautiful, so wise, and so filled with integrity. So many of them live in nuttiness that is beyond their control, yet they are intact, they are doing the best they can to survive.

Katie Crane – 17 years old *(See page 129 Colour Insert)*

Grandson,
hope your Christmas is happy...

Dear   we hope you have
a Happy Christmas and happy
birthday to. focus more on your
future, Graupa don't like to
have losers. Love Grauma
                    + Graupa.

Abraham – 14 years old

1. Illusion Vs Truth – The Role Of Parents

A few years ago, I attended a grade seven school- leaving banquet for all the grade sevens and their parents. The oldest kids in that school were moving up to the high school in September where they would become the youngest. The school principal addressed the audience, everyone dressed to the nines, all arranged in named seating at the banquet tables. The gym was nicely decorated to mark the occasion. After welcoming everyone, the principal began his speech by solemnly looking across the tables and launching into a personal exhortation that all the kids were sitting next to the best friends that they would ever have in the world, their parents. He went on to explain how they had been nurtured, guided, supported, and loved. He told them how none of their friends would ever match this and that they owed their parents a unique level of respect.

Meanwhile, just up from me, sat a petite, blonde girl in a light blue dress. Her hair was tied back and she looked up at the principal as intently as all the rest of the kids. But I could see her every so often quickly turning her head to scan the entrance door. Next to her were two empty seats with name placards propped above them on the table. I wondered where her best friends were.

Then, just as the principal finished, in walked two adults in biker leathers who made their way to the empty seats. Not biker leathers as in biker gang or hard cases. Biker leathers as in clueless. Biker leathers as in "I don't give a damn, we were out for a ride, what's the big deal anyway." The blonde girl's shoulders slumped a bit, but her mouth smiled. I imagined the array of emotions that must have been swirling within her. She was, of course, relieved that they had gotten there, happy to see mom and her boyfriend, angry that they had arrived so late, embarrassed that they had dressed the way they had so absolutely different then everyone else, and determined not to let anyone else in on any of this.

In actuality, the principal had it all backwards. He should more accurately have told the parents assembled that the best friends they would ever have in the world were sitting next to them, namely their kids. It is the child who keeps loving despite the disappointments, despite the inadequacies, the selfishnesses, the neglect, and the abuses of his parents.

SAMUEL - I learned this especially deeply from a 13 year old named Samuel. He was a grade eight student, and right from the get go, he was driving his teachers nuts. Instead of studiously sitting in class, taking notes, and raising his hand to speak, he was chatting with friends, making smart-assed comments when the teacher was talking, and just generally disrupting the lesson. Everyone knew he was smart, but they found him unmanageable. I had heard the rumblings and seen him visiting the vice-principal's office on occasion. We finally became acquainted directly when my door opened one day and the French teacher, a well-liked and normally gregarious, positive woman flung Samuel into my office. She was livid, and all she said was, "Here, you take him!" She slammed the door and went back to her classroom, probably with a mixture of ahhhhh... and self-recrimination.

So there was Samuel and I alone together. He also was pretty steamed. Being yarded down the length of the hallway from the far end of the school likely wasn't what he had planned for his afternoon's French class. Yet, within a few moments, he had calmed down, and began to impress me with his clear articulation. He knew full well that he was a lot to handle, and he had no problem admitting his responsibility for this latest hubbub. What he was irked at was why the teacher had reacted so extremely when his behaviour hadn't really been much different than it normally was. He had felt surprised and embarrassed she had been other than her usual tolerant self. Then we proceeded to get to know each other.

By the end of that first session, it was pretty clear that Samuel suffered from Attention Deficit Disorder. He had tried medication but didn't like it and refused to try it again. More importantly, I started to learn about his home life.

Samuel lived alone with his father Brian. His mom lived 500 miles away in another city. She was a professional working in an office. His dad was a jack of all trades, doing one thing for awhile to make a buck and then switching to something else when that dried up. And Brian was an alcoholic.

Through the course of many visits with Samuel, in an effort to try to assist him to manage his behaviour in class so that he could achieve grades reflective of his ability and so that he didn't get expelled, I learned more about his dad and their life together. Brian was a real blowhard and show-off. He liked to be the centre of attention. He, too, was relatively smart but had never gone further in school than grade 12. Samuel found his father's drinking hard to take, and he especially found it difficult when Brian occasionally didn't come home at night. He worried about him. During those times he would phone his father's former live-in girlfriend, with whom Samuel had felt an accepting bond. She had been out of their family picture for some time and was now in another relationship, but in the same town. She was always supportive.

Some of Samuel's peers were not so supportive. Because he could be mouthy and clever with his comments some of the kids in the next grade would go after him. Samuel had a few good friends, but, more often than not, he had to watch his back and be ready to run. In some ways, he liked the adrenaline of it. As with his classroom antics, negative attention was better than none at all, and Samuel needed to feel some kind of control in his life. If he could be responsible for the attention he got because he knew how to push people's buttons, well, that was a useful salve to the helplessness he felt over his father's behaviour and the disappearance of nurturing women from his life. And of course, his dad was a fitting model of how to behave.

It was Brian's drinking that led Samuel to ask me to call his father in so the three of us could talk and tackle how the booze was affecting Samuel. After a bit of nervous tension, we began the meeting. He had no idea what the topic was to be, but to his credit rather than go into any denial, Brian started crying when confronted about his drinking and tearfully declared how he loved his son and would cut down. Samuel was moved by his dad's assertions, and he appreciated being told that he did matter.

Brian likely never did cut down all that much, but it was shortly after that meeting when the Ministry of Children's Services got involved. Samuel had previously told me how he and his father had, in the past, gotten into physical fights. This hadn't happened for some months. In some ways, it was a power struggle between a teen who couldn't stand the inconsistencies and haughty aberrations of his dad, and the latter's frustrations that his son was both rebelling and, in his own mind, behaving obnoxiously. In one of the fights, Brian had bitten Samuel. If the fighting wasn't over the line, the biting was truly bizarre.

Anyway, in a phone conversation with his mother, Samuel had mentioned the biting. She had known they had fought in the past, but hadn't known it had taken that kind of turn. So, when she heard about it, she phoned the Ministry. The same day, a social worker had pulled Samuel from his home and put him in temporary foster care. That the incident had taken place months before didn't seem to matter. In my own conversation with the social worker, I could see she was on her own personal mission to show this father what he could and couldn't do. She was going to save the boy and show the dad who was boss.

Samuel was flabbergasted that he had been snatched from his home and put in a strange new place. He had not had any inkling something like that was about to transpire. He was even more upset at being told he could have no contact with his father.

After a week of this without knowing when or if he would ever get to go home, Samuel came into my office a nervous wreck. He missed his father intensely. All he wanted was to go home to this man who had failed him in so many ways. And he wanted to be sure he was okay. As he was pacing and yelling in my office, I asked him if he wanted a hug, which I had never reason to venture before. I shall never forget the look on his face as he instantly said, yeah. And I shall not forget how tightly he held on and for how long.

The two opposite extremities in the range of parents are the viciously abusive (or literally non-existent parents), and the involved and loving parents who, within themselves, feel self-loving and complete. Most of us fall somewhere in between. Yet, too many of us adults are either not sufficiently grown up or have not sufficiently had our own needs met. We focus too much on what *we* want rather than on what our kids need and deserve. Thus, we enter or leave relationships, move to different towns, set rules, and act out all according to our own moods or self-centred impulses. We do this because we are so often driven by getting our own needs met, and because we know we can get away with it. We know our kids need us and we've learned, either consciously or unconsciously - perhaps through our own experience growing up - that they will accept us and want us regardless of our behaviour.

This isn't to say that a "good" parent only does what their kids want. It just means that a "good" parent truly takes into consideration what is in the best interests of their kids and blends that with what else is happening. It means that decisions made by the parent are made on the basis of the collective self, not the individual self. In other words the parent doesn't think in terms of "what I want" but in terms of "what will work best for all of us." Of course, none of us can do this all the time or maybe not even most of the time, but we can aim for it, we can be conscious of it.

Instead, so often we automatically prioritize our own needs and, in so doing, limit our perception and analysis. Thus, for instance we may feel a growing distance or disenchantment with our spouse, and we begin to fixate on whether or not we should end the relationship. Maybe we would be happier with someone else. If we saw it as a collective situation, we would be more inclined to see it as "How can I fix this? What do I need to do to make it better?" Again, this does not mean sacrificing oneself and becoming a martyr by staying in an abusive or empty relationship for the sake of an intact family. Indeed some relationships are empirically toxic and the kids suffer from that toxicity. They are better served by the parents splitting, and the sooner the better.

LOUISE - Louise and her mother snuck out of their house at midnight for just that reason. With suitcases packed, they ran across the fields to reach the road in order to make their way to a friend's home. Father was at home passed out. He was a constantly irrational man. There was always tension in the house. He had beaten her mother in the past, and she had threatened to leave but had never gone through with it. At last, Louise was experiencing her mother's capacity to act, to take care of the well-being of both of them. Her mother didn't know any other way to do it.

Louise was in grade 12. She had vague sensations that her father had sexually abused her - fondled her in the bed sometime when she was a few years younger, though she had no clarity, couldn't be sure. Louise was saddened that her home was irrevocably changing, that she would never again have both her parents. And she was sad to leave her dad behind. Despite everything, she loved him and wished him well.

In fact, in the months after they made their exit, she came into my office one day in a real panic. She hadn't heard from or seen her dad in days and had picked up some signs that he might be suicidal. She begged me to do something to help him. We phoned a relative to ask him to intervene.

But, regardless of her love and her sadness that night of the leaving, above it all Louise felt a deep sense of relief. She felt like she could breathe and that her life could expand and go forward with less stress. She was fully ready to take the loss.

So, of course, some relationships should end and some families need to uproot and move their kids across the continent due to work conditions. But, far too often, it comes down to the adults serving their own impulses and not giving the needs of their kids full due in their deliberations.

The teen years are when kids individuate. For their own maturation and independent development, they need to emotionally and ideologically separate from their parents. This natural process happens whether they have strong, healthy relationships with their parents or distant, weak, or dysfunctional ones. Their peer groups take on a huge importance. In those instances, when the prior emotional attachment with their parents has been either lacking or disrupted, the peer bond can become problematic depending on the character of that peer group. I'll discuss this more later on. First, I want to emphasize that the developmental separation that takes place does not mean that parents lose their value for the teens. Inside they still need and want the same degree of love from their parents, it's just that their interests and emotional changes are facing them towards peers. Thus, they need to spend more time with their friends. It's not that their parents don't mean so much to them.

Teens often don't see themselves very clearly. They don't understand their own inner workings. Their lives are a mix of ruminating on their own issues and stimulations and just getting out there everyday to interact. Go into the hallways of any school in the country, and the energy and activity will look and sound the same. Eavesdrop on conversations at the lunch tables, read the text messages, even examine the postures of our teens. It's all one homogenous entity. They're all the same. Each school has its jocks, its preps, its nerds, its brainiacs, its goths, and its fringies. You could teleport any one or one group of them to a school two thousand kilometres away and in a few days they'd feel fully at home, finding a familiar niche.

Inside, they just want to feel good. They want their parents to be happy. They want to have two parents at home. They want their parents to love each other and to love them. If they have siblings they want that everyone should get along together. They want to be accepted by their peers and they want friends. They want to be happy and successful. And they want to find someone who will love them and who they love. Yet, their behaviours and attitudes may not reflect any of this.

This all complicates the making of rules. It's easy to make rules for kids when they are little. Bed time, going out, friendships, purchases, chores, you name it, when the parent makes the rule, with very few exceptions the child complies. They know who the boss is and they like to please the boss. It's all accepted as the natural order.

As each year of teen life progresses, the aware parent adjusts the rules. Two significant factors play into the setting of those rules. One, parents usually want to control their kids, this being driven both by concern for proper development and by awareness of what others will think. Two, parents aren't sure what exactly is appropriate. The kids, of course, only know what they want and what their friends are getting. So they generally try to get that by hook or by crook.

The teen years are when the real arguments start, and they inevitably start over the rules. Teens are no longer in the relative safety net of grade school and the watchful eyes of doting teachers. They are now expected to get things done and run their own affairs at school. Homework increases hugely, teachers demand more, peers have become more powerful, and the high school community is a state on its own in which everyone must find their own mode of survival. So, logically, they want and expect more freedom from their parents.

This is the time of alcohol and drugs, of parties and relationships. As a norm of teenage life, most teens feel the need to get into the swing of all that. And even if they are not so inclined they will want to have their own space and time. For the first time, parents will hear the words, "Don't tell me what to do," followed by "You never.....," and punctuated by the never ending, "Why?"

Whenever I counsel both parents and kids in the same room, I always aim at reaching a compromise. I try to get the kid to see it from the parent's point of view and vice versa. Having a neutral third party usually helps them to actually hear each other. Kids know they need limits and they expect the parents to set them. Despite their protests, they don't mind as much as it might seem. Parents, on the other hand, are not necessarily so aware of their kid's need to do their own thing.

One regularly hears ominous voice-overs on television especially during the summer, "Do you know where your kids are?" As much as parents want that exact knowledge, there is no way they can accurately have it all the time. The best that can be hoped for is that the teen has an internal governance functioning that will limit the precariousness of their behaviour. A basic fact of the teenage years is that teens do not tell their parents the truth, certainly not all of it.

JERRY - Jerry's parents were at their wits end because of Jerry's lying. It drove them nuts. They didn't want him smoking. He told them he wasn't, and then they found out he was. They told him to stay home when they were going out. He took off right after they left, and later denied it. After going to bed, he'd sneak out the window and visit friends.

This persistent behaviour was tearing the family apart. Jerry felt bad about lying, but he craved his freedom and the right to make his own decisions, right or wrong. His parents wanted him to be a good boy. They wanted to trust him. They wanted him to be the way they wanted him to be.

I could easily see that they needed to let up. They needed to figure out in their own minds what they considered essential behaviour and what they were prepared to let go of. My one goal was to stop Jerry from lying. That's how I discovered a rather unorthodox solution. I instructed the parents to stop asking Jerry questions about his behaviour. If they didn't ask then he wouldn't need to lie. And I instructed Jerry that he had to solemnly promise not to initiate a lie. I explained that initiating a lie was deception, and as such, it was aggression. If he was angry at his parents and wanted to show them, I suggested he find another way other than initiating a lie to deceive them.

So, it was theoretically solved if both parties complied. By not asking questions they would not be lied to. If Jerry kept his word, he would have his privacy without the guilt of being dishonest. Needless to say, the parents didn't embrace this with much vigor. How could they know what he was up to if they didn't ask? They rightly argued that Jerry wasn't going to volunteer that he was smoking or drinking or sneaking out. How could they maintain structure and order? Where would the discipline be?

My response was that as it was, he was smoking, drinking, sneaking out, and sundry other debatable behaviours, plus he was lying about it. So, we could at least eliminate one of the transgressions and one that seemed to irk them the most. And, I added, Jerry lied because he knew his parents were too over-bearing. He didn't have a chance to make his own mind up. He was too busy calculating how to escape and thwart their controls. By not always interrogating and suspiciously and constantly checking up on him, maybe Jerry would come to more of a balance. Maybe Jerry would start thinking about and evaluating some of his own choices. At times, that is what some space allows.

It's vital that parents clearly articulate their expectations. They need to do this regularly. It's vital that parents explain their own standards and values, not skimping on the how they came to those conclusions. It's vital that parents give regular feedback to their teens on how they see things in the teen's life, how they assess their kid's choices, friends, activities. And they should feel free to tell them precisely what they want. Then they need to add the most powerful qualifier of all. They need to add that they understand that their teen will make their own mind up.

That way, the kid gets the full value of their parents' analysis and guidance - this from the ones who have raised them and know them better than anyone else in the world.

In turn, the kid gets the recognition and affirmation that it is their life and they have their own mind. Doing this makes it more likely that the teen will reflect more deeply and thoughtfully on their own choices and behaviours. This reflection is what is paramount to developing successful independence. Instead of pushing willy-nilly ahead, insisting on it being "my own life", and letting peer influence or rebellion be the power behind choices and behaviour, teens might start their own checking and balancing based on the offered guidance they have internalized from their parents.

A father I know watched his 16 year old daughter several times go in and out of a relationship with the same 17 year old boy. They'd become arduous, fight, split up, and then he'd find a way to win her back, and the pattern would start over again. Finally, after they had gotten back together for the third time, he stepped in and took his daughter aside. He bluntly told her that he didn't want her to stay in the relationship. He said he had watched her go up and down like a yo-yo over many months, said he saw how unhappy she had often been, how volatile and mixed up he thought her boyfriend was, and said that, as her father, he didn't want her getting hurt anymore or living with such turbulence. Then he said the key words: "I know you will do what you want to do, but I just want you to know what I think as someone who has loved you from the moment you were born."

His daughter, being the 16 year old she was, immediately replied with indignation that he couldn't make her do that and added that he couldn't tell her who she could or couldn't be with. Her father didn't react to her defensiveness, but instead looked her in the eyes and said calmly, "I know that. I'm not trying to make you do anything and I'm not telling you what to do. I'm honestly telling you what $\underline{I}$ want and why, and I'm telling you what I think is best for you. Don't you think that's what a good parent should do? I know you will make your own mind up, and I know it's your decision. I just wanted to tell you how I saw it and what I want." The daughter blinked and didn't have a clue how to respond. The dad was not trying to put any pressure on her, not trying to control her.

A week later she broke up with the boy and they never got back together again.

I am over flooded
with emotion
I am more upset
than ever, this
is the best feeling
I have felt in a long
time, I am un-aware
I have no control
of my emotion, I
finally feel a little
more like a kid.

KRIS - 15 YRS
OLD.

Teens need to know what their parents think and why. Parents need to know what their kids think and why. They each need to understand as clearly as possible where each are coming from. And they need to know what each wants. This results in giving the parents as much control and involvement as is healthily possible and increases the likelihood of the teen making good decisions.

It's normal and quite okay for teens to have secrets. This is simple privacy. They don't talk or act with their friends the same as they would if their parents were present. Parents need to let this be. It's okay for teens to screw up. They need to screw up. One of the top students in my school, and a top teacher's son to boot, got drunk at a school dance and received a suspension. His dad was angry and embarrassed. The behaviour was uncustomary for the boy. Other teachers shook their heads in dismay. He was sent to me for counselling. I got him to tell me all about it, what led up to it, how he felt now about it, what his relationship with alcohol was, how he had handled his parents' reaction. Then I told him I thought it was good that he screwed up. It was good for him to be the bad boy for a change, to be less than excellent, to be diminished in others' eyes. Now he could identify with others a bit more. Now he could see himself as just a kid like other kids. He could cut himself some slack, learn from this, and breathe a bit more easily. He thought about it, smiled and nodded his head.

He never got suspended again nor ever drank at another dance, but I'm sure he still drinks alcohol on occasion, and he's now a psychologist in professional sports.

As parents, we worry about our kids holding secrets from us. Instead of demanding to know, instead of conveying how much we distrust their readiness to act wisely or how much we distrust them, which in turn makes them less confident or more rebellious, we need to support them. Let them have that privacy. Ask how we can help, what they need for support. And listen to their answers. We need to ask how the rules fit for them, and if they think they are fair and reasonable.

ANJIOUX - Too much control almost always brings about just what we fear the most. The oddest example of parents being so hung up on control that I ever encountered was the case in which a couple were bugging their daughter Anjioux's telephone. They had already read her diary and found out she had been sexual with a boy. That so startled them, filled them with such panic, that they immediately confronted her, grounded her, and secretly put a tape on her phone.

In my office, the mother had been beside herself with exasperation that her daughter had performed fellatio on a boy - according to the diary. She exclaimed with frantic, wide eyes to her daughter, "How could you do such a thing?! It's so dirty. Don't you respect yourself at all?" Obviously, mom could never see herself voluntarily doing such an act. I didn't bother looking over at the dad during this conversation, but I must admit, I was tempted.

We live in an age when sexuality, perhaps, has less bounds than ever before in history. Kids are not particularly averse to experimenting. Visually, the naked body has never been more accessible. All sexual acts have become visible and normalized on the internet. This is both good and bad. Good, in that physical bodies are desirable, they are fun, and they make us feel good. Kids should feel free to explore each other more will be said on that later. So, the teen girl was potentially engaging in acceptable, healthy behaviour. Of course, it might have been otherwise, depending on the girl's self-esteem, maturity and motivation, the nature of the boy, and the circumstances. None of this was of any concern to the mother, however. The act of fellatio, simply in itself, was a horrendous, shameful taboo.

The girl was horrified for the mother to know, to have read her diary, and to be blurting it out in front of the school counsellor. If ever there was a chance for her parents to influence her sexual choices, it had just evaporated. The parents' goal was to get their daughter to be who they wanted her to be. In order to achieve this, they felt the need to know everything.

Privately, I urged them to cease bugging their daughter's telephone. I explained how it violated her rights, was voyeuristic, and blatantly wrong for them to do it. Mother was patient with my exhortation, and calmly replied, "Yes, but we have to. Otherwise, we won't know what she's doing." End of discussion. They had five younger sons, and Amrita was the lone girl.

I later tried to indelibly impress to the girl that she needed to no longer discuss private issues on the telephone. I looked her in the eyes intently and asserted, "If you talk about private things on your phone, I guarantee you that your parents will find out." I couldn't be more explicit than that. Thus is the school counsellor's adherence to confidentiality and not burning bridges. She never presumed a tape on her phone, but I think she got the message as I never heard anything more from her parents. I do know that the girl resolved to go about her business with far greater secrecy, and that she no longer had the utility of a diary for sorting out her own inner thoughts.

Parents often worry about their kids seeing a counsellor. They worry that the family secrets will be exposed. They also worry that the counsellor will hear a one-sided story. It isn't difficult to discern the nervousness or suspicion that parents harbour when they know I am visiting with their offspring. This is especially true if there are issues at home which aren't healthy, or if it is very important for the parents' self-image or reputation to be perceived as upstanding and successful. In our society, we have always held on to the notion that struggle is a flaw or an indication of weakness. A good family has no problems. A good parent knows everything about her kids. In a good family, the kids tell their parents whenever something is wrong. Going outside for help is a sign of failure. Odd that we don't hold the same standard over medical, legal, mechanical, plumbing, heavy lifting, or any other issue. In all those cases, it's natural and desirable to get the best assistance. We don't even think twice. Yet when it comes to emotional or family struggles, we slink into a wall of denial or secrecy.

In some cases, the parents do have something to hide. Substance abuse, family violence, physical, emotional, or sexual abuse are, by definition, in need of hiding. Otherwise, it is more logical for parents to feel relieved that their kids are talking to someone about their lives. It adds another plank to the emotional development of that child. It means the child is taking responsibility to address and resolve their difficulties. It means their kid is going to do okay.

Every counsellor knows that what they hear from a client is that client's story, that client's version of events. When a teen expounds on the terrible stuff at home or with their friends, it's the teen's version, the teen's understanding. It isn't the empirical truth, though at any given time it could be. The counsellor's job is to help the teen make sense of what they are experiencing and perceiving. This is done by first validating what is being espoused and then prompting for more explanation, more examination of the details, more precise exploration of exactly what is being experienced, what is being felt, what conclusions are being drawn. Thereby, the story evolves and the client's understanding evolves. The impact changes. Adaptations, empowerment, growth occurs. All parents ought to want this for their kids.

ZITS

"Ahhh, Grrr"
they have struck
once again

the troopers
that march
without fail

the army
that
intrudes my pores

they fear
not
the cream
nor
the soap

It's their
Destiny
to conquer MY FACE

Rosa Smedley – 13 years old

MEMORY

My mother and I were over at her boyfriend Bob's. They were drinking a little bit and we were all just having a good time together. It was Christmas Eve and I always get to open one present. I opened a new belt that I was begging my mother for and I was really happy that I got it. Her boyfriend wanted to show me something with it. He folded it in half and made a big snapping sound. He did this about six times and he broke it. I cried all that night. I was about 5 I think.

This made me very sad inside because I really wanted that belt.

My mother isn't strong like she used to be. She is abusing herself. She can't make herself better. She's putting stress on me.

I wish my dad would come back from Edmonton.

This makes me hate myself and hate her. Which makes me mad at myself.

Stasia – 14 years old

2. Are They Doing It?

This is a biggie for most parents. No one wants their kid getting pregnant or getting someone else pregnant. Less of a concern, no one wants their kid with an STD. Lesser yet, but still significant, no parent wants their kid to be promiscuous. The smartest, most functional parents need to have these concerns. So, instead of hoping for the best, they need to be proactive. I remember my own mother pulling the car over when I was 13 or 14 and, in great seriousness, asking me if I knew about the birds and the bees yet. I shrunk in my seat, answered tersely that I did, and that was the end of it.

Because of the sexual minefield we have created and continue to expand on, it has never been more crucial for parents to be involved with their teenagers' sexual attitudes and practices. Not in the fashion of the mom who was mortified at her daughter's oral sex, but in the fashion of a caregiver who is more experienced and who needs to be a guide. It might be embarrassing or uncomfortable. It might be difficult to know how to create the communication. Get over it. It's too important. There is nothing wrong with embarrassment and nothing wrong with fumbling for words. Fortify yourself with the truism that your teens need your guidance. They need your input. When they don't have it, then they are getting it from trial and error, from peer pressure, from the internet, and from their buddies. None of this is adequate and, in some cases, disastrous. For the parents, it means, at best, a blind fingers crossed hope that nothing painful happens. At worst, it means everyone suffers.

The first step is for parents to start talking about sex with each other. Start talking with other parents about sex in the current time. Start reading up on what healthy sexuality is.

I'll offer my opinions on it. If you disagree, that's fine, just make sure you have solid, objective reasons that can make sense in today's world, and that your own opinions are practical.

I think sexual experience is a gift. Theoretically, I think that it's okay for teenagers to have sex with each other. The huge qualifier is that they need to know what it means, and they need to know themselves well enough to make the decision. Few are in this category.

It is different for males and females because of the gender roles we've imprinted. At first glance, males would seem to have the easier lot. Just as women have had to fight for centuries to achieve close to equality, so, too, their sexuality has been bludgeoned. It is no great mystery why female genital mutilation is practiced today in more than a few countries. Sexual women as much as they turn men on, scare the crap out of them. They are viewed with fear, distrust, and suspicion of infidelity. A good woman is a chaste woman or a faithful girlfriend or wife. This old tale plays out daily in the social alleyways of our schools. Word gets around very quickly.

A girl who has sex is a girl with a reputation. It is not as constrained as it used to be. Teens can be quite forgiving, quite accepting, and are certainly more embracing of change than adults. And they have a sharp sense for injustice or equality, so a sexually active girl is not the slut she was a decade ago. Still, to be safe, a girl keeps her activity hidden and knows the social risk of sexual behaviour. Unless she is in a serious, committed relationship, her sexual choices will be open to judgment.

More than anything, the one aspect that hasn't changed is the presumption that the girl gives her body, that it is the boy who "gets lucky". The male orgasm and the boy's quest to achieve it is the driver in the sexual exchange.

By and large, girls have been estranged from their own sexuality. This cannot be overstated. Everyone grows up with the powerful image of what a good mother is, and that's definitely not someone brimming with sexuality. Moms are branded as asexual. So the same sex children grow up modeling this detachment from sexuality. Moms who do display overt sexuality risk raised eyebrows, gossip, and finger pointing at best. Daughters unconsciously internalize this. Sons of mothers who are sexual bear discomfort and uneasiness. One young boy talked to me in my office about hearing his mom having sex with a man. His conclusion – "I thought she was a slut."

Daughters also learn that men covet women for sex. They buy girlie books or ogle women on the street. Daughters have fathers and those fathers are men. So, how does the daughter then accept or make sense of her own developing sexuality and sexual interests?

Simple anatomy also enters into it. Boys can stick their penises where they want and scamper off, body untouched. Girls have to open themselves up to be entered. So much riskier and more vulnerable. Compounded by the lingering notion that they're not supposed to be doing that or to be wanting that. Girls are told to save themselves. They know what a slut is, what a good girl is, and what their parents want of them. Boys are spared all of this.

More precisely, girls are not given permission to have pursuit of an orgasm as a core component of their sexual activity. This is unfortunate, because sexuality can be such a strong grounding for a person's sense of self. The genital is in the centre of the body. Being consciously involved in obtaining sexual pleasure is a statement of self-worth. It is an affirmation of one's place on the planet. It means acceptance of who one is.

When our bodies are connected to our thoughts and feelings, we function better. This is why schools need to teach about the positives of masturbation. Parents and school-based sex education classes should be gulping and getting this simple directive out there. Masturbation is such a positive statement to self, and developing female teenagers need as many of these as they can get. Masturbation says, "I'm a girl, I have sexual feelings, and I deserve to explore and release these feelings in privacy and under my own control."

This latter point is so important. There are no social consequences, no judgments risked, no rejections, no peer pressure, no "I thought he loved me's". The experience is solely under the girl's control. Risk free and a happy, confidence boosting, physically infusing event, a masturbated orgasm tells her that it's good to be alive that day.

Alone in the safety of her bedroom and exploring the sensations, unhurriedly learning about her body reactions, there need be no guilt, no worry, no doubt about her right to do this or the various sensations or feelings or ideas that result. She is by herself, safe and under the affirmation that her body solely belongs to her and that all the physical, sensual responses in it are hers. An affirmation that says, this is the way to intimacy with oneself, a way to know oneself and accept oneself. Enjoy it. Learn from it.

Now, think about how this then translates to relationships with others. Will it build towards an identity based on self-confidence, equality, and respect and thus increase the chances for equal and full relationships with a partner? Or will it decrease all of that?

What about the pornography and sexual tsunami that flies at us from the outside world here in the West? Will this girl be more grounded and more self-aware of her own rights and sexuality so as to see through the shallowness, exploitation and objectification? Or less so?

Most of us are totally intimidated to broach the subject of masturbation with our teen girls. We consider it private, too sensitive, or taboo. It's time we get over it and think of the girl's best interests. There is no hesitation to discuss condoms and even demonstrate how to use them by putting a condom on a banana. Female counsellors in every school should be introducing and teaching about masturbation, giving it legitimacy and air. Instead, we prattle on about STD's, about HIV/AIDS, and about pregnancy. We feel free to talk about what to avoid, but offer no guidance on what to aim for, on how to respond to sexuality.

As part of various family life courses, female teens in so many schools spend a 24 hour stint with a mechanical, simulated baby in order to get the point of what a job it is to have one. The baby cries, wets itself, and is always there. The hope is the kid will think twice about having sex and, especially, unprotected sex. Condoms are offered. Abstinence is suggested. I remember one community gathering to discuss a student council's intent to put condom machines in the school washrooms. An almost tearful mom got up and addressed the audience, and particularly the female students in attendance. She pled for them to not give away the flower of their virginity, but, instead, to save it as a precious gift for their future husbands.

The problem is that, in our over-sexualized world, the opposite message is coming through a million times more loudly. Saying no may be an option for a certain percentage of girls, but, even then, it ought not be at the cost of a skewed sense of body or sexuality. The bottom line is that kids and all of us need to embrace our own sexuality, need to feel only positive about it. We need an untainted relationship with our own bodies, our own genitals, and our own sexuality.

In this regard, I think we also ought to be including a "what to do and how to do it" section in our sex education classes. Right now kids are getting all their direction from the internet, from movies, and from their friends. They are encountering all these created scenarios, which stem from the adult world's desire to make money. Pornography is ubiquitous; it's mainstream. Virtually every teenager will have watched or seen explicit sexual images by the time they leave school. Too often, on a regular basis. As such, they are schooling themselves on sexuality, how to be sexual, what to want, what to expect, and what to demand. All of it is false, it's mind shaping, and it's male focused. Women are objects. Sex is an object. It's all about stimulation and gratification.

Isn't this a problem? When our kids are getting their instructions and their understanding of intimacy from a source, the only purpose of which is to exploit, isn't that something that we need to change?

Our sex education classes should start talking about sexual intimacy in straightforward and complete detail. We need to normalize love, respect, nervousness, communication, emotional warmth, and being consciously connected to one's body as being central to sexual sharing. A grade seven girl was flagged as having a hard edge, as being more sexually mature than her peers, and as having home problems. She had openly referred to her mother as being a MILF. For the uninitiated, it means A Mother I'd Like To F... I'll let you fill in the blanks. It's a term prevalent on internet pornography sites and the concept was popularized in the teen sex movie "American Pie".

So, we can know exactly how inundated our kids are with sexual modeling and guidance from all the superficial and profit driven purveyors and do nothing about it, or we **can** take control of the situation and offer a direct and wise alternative. We **can** be the primary source of their sexual knowledge. We **can** start talking about what to do when you climb into bed naked with someone. About penises being hard and clitorises being hard and labia being swollen. We **can** talk about going slow, about touching, listening, paying attention, asking, feeling one's feelings. We **can** talk about orgasms. We **can** talk about lubrication, positions, oral sex, and having fun with a partner. We **can** talk about exploration and how it is good and proper, that girls should initiate everything just as much as boys should and that it doesn't cast a pall on character. Discussion **can** centre on the issue of respect and what it entails, why it's the foundation for sexual relations, and how its core tenet of mutuality is so vital. That it's okay not to have sex, to not be ready, to not want to engage in specific acts ever, or at any particular moment and for any particular reason, and that more pressure is not an okay response. And we **should** talk about masturbation!

The deeper that we jump into the whole area of sex education, the better. The internet has total hold right now, and it covers everything that's on the surface - everything. The sex merchants continuously work at devising every possible sexual schema and interaction so as to continuously attract and keep customers. Appetites are thus created that never before existed. It is possible to view every manner of sexual deviance and degradation. Opening a sex site inevitably leads one on a trail to ever more trails. This is the private world of our children. There is little chance they won't find their way onto these sites and in so doing absorb details, behaviour, and imagery that will stay with them and influence them.

In the old days, sex magazines sold in the corner store had restrictive measures. Pubic areas were not shown. That curtailment ended. Then it was prohibition of depiction of sexual acts. That went by the wayside. Now, most reputable stores have their sex magazines either higher in the shelves and/or with the pictures on their covers obscured by a wrapper. Movies bear restricted ratings where no one under the age of 18 is allowed in. All fine and well, but to no real avail. Kids can watch old men having sex with babies on their cell phones any time they want. They can watch animals and women. They can watch group orgies complete with ejaculation after ejaculation. As soon as a sex merchant can think of a new scenario, it will be on the internet and in the eyes of our children.

To think that kids will not see any of this is neglectful thinking. Curiosity and natural hormonal development coupled with peer influence will outweigh parental directives nine times out of ten. The imagery and the videos available in full colour on the internet are indelible teaching tools. In response, we, the mature leaders and care givers of our children, talk mechanically, indirectly, selectively and with great nervousness and hesitancy about sex and their sexuality. It's like whispering to someone in the midst of a rock concert. What will the person hear?

The sex education offered in schools in the 1970's was in the context of a society that still had limits and restrictions. Today, sexual exposure is limitless. Our kids live in this reality, but the sex education that they receive in school is the same as that offered in the 1970's. The adult world just doesn't get it. The disconnect from the reality of our teens is too immense.

JANINE AND KELSA - These two girls, fifteen and sixteen years old respectively, spent an afternoon educating me about their world. They introduced me to the term, "Two Girls, One Cup". They introduced me to scads of YouTube clips, the focus of which was audience or individual reaction to viewing "Two Girls, One Cup". The most popular clip had well over six and a half million hits. The others also in the many millions. Not only is it the case of viral watching of explicit, sexual depravity, but viral watching of others watching the depravity!

So, what is "Two Girls, One Cup"? It is pornography involving a naked woman having her buttocks held apart by another woman as she defecates into a cup. The holding woman licks at the excrement as it drops.

Janine and Kelsa explained that all teens know of that scenario. And many more scenarios. Obviously, the kids aren't coming home to tell mom or dad, "Hi, guess what I've been watching?" This is the hidden world our kids inhabit. Janine told me how "everyone watches pornography now, all the guys and most chicks." She related how older boys, especially recent graduates, have accessed pornography and then introduce it to younger friends and the girls in their lives. The result, in Janine's words, is the creating of visual memories of what sex is supposed to be. She was adamant that "her generation was really exploited".

The girls talked of how boys now expect from girls what they see in the visuals. The stimulation from the pornography is transferred into real life and onto the relations that the boys have with girls. Thus it is that young teens gather at parties and two girls are prodded and enticed into making out together for the titillation of the group. A girl and boy engage in sex in front of everyone for the same titillation. This all mimics what they've seen on the internet or in popular videos such as "Girls Gone Wild".

The depersonalizing of sexual behaviour and the normalizing of acting out what's been seen extends to sharing experiences. Janine and Kelsa related how usual it is for boys to disclose what they've done with girls. This influences others into presuming normalcy and common practice.

Adults can bleat about morals, choices and upbringing, but those have become empty words. They no longer reflect any active process for an ever increasing proportion of our population. As Kelsa said, "It all depends on the environment that you grow up in. If your parents are actively and fully discussing sexuality with you, then maybe you have a chance to make decisions."

What is the consequence for these developing beings who watch or participate in these kinds of no limits sexual behaviours? Inevitably, they force the teen to disassociate. The child splits away from the emotional impact of their experience. The kid becomes two – the inner person, which is in emotional turmoil or fragility, and the outer, image person. The teen struggles to stay on the surface, stay away from the inner emotions and confusion. Their consequent brashness or superficial, all-is-fine appearance is all an act. The need to fit in with a group, the desire to be wanted or cool, or simply have attention, combines with the power of the pornographic tsunami to lure kids into harmful behavior and attitudes. This is self damaging and certainly growth limiting. Our kids are in a pandemic, and it will only get worse until adults become accountable for their failure to respond.

Our fear should not be our excuse for giving over the sexual education of our children to the sex merchants. I realize that younger kids are already infected with the adult world of sexuality, but there needs to be a line, and, by grade eight, there is enough intellectual development and maturity to introduce realistic sexual themes. By thirteen most kids are into puberty. So that seems to be a good age. Some might argue for it to start in grade five or six.

The teaching groups should allow for adult presentation and for peer discussion. Orgasms are a particularly sensitive topics for adults it seems. But since orgasms drive most males, it's a smart idea to get the kids introduced to the subject early. Take the secrecy and the taboo out of it. Boys snicker about sex. Comedians fill the air with jokes about sex. Nudge, nudge, wink, wink. The internet tells us we need to graduate from this reluctance. Boys need our guidance. Girls need our permission.

For boys, we need to help them understand orgasms as not the end all and be all of their quest. They need to be given the lens of intimacy with which to understand their ejaculation and release. They need to be given the lens of respect and recognition of other. They need to have the limited lens of physicality and being the doer replaced by the lens of emotional and personal depth and mutuality. That's why we need to engage teens in the discussion of intimacy. We need to guide them to an understanding of how touch and closeness, loving and risking are the soul of sexuality, and that the physical sensations are just that - physical. We need to illuminate for them that sex is pleasurable and stress releasing, that these are good and their rights, but that the deeper truth is that sex is a doorway to themselves, to the truth of other, to an intimacy that puts us more firmly on the planet. These distinctions must be brought into their consciousness.

As with the earlier comments on masturbation, girls need to see their orgasms as the natural and logical conclusion to their intimacy and giving. They need up front articulation and recognition from adults that orgasms belong to them. That they are as much their right as breathing is.

As for the boys, their sexuality also has been skewed. "It's a man's world", wasn't coined in error. The "head of the family" too often grows up with an overriding sense of entitlement. Inside, any male may have suffered all manner of hurt or trauma, but along with that will be the imprint of entitlement. A boy takes what he wants. Aggressiveness is prized and rewarded. We see it in business, in sports, and in government. We call males who aren't assertive enough, "pussies". Since boys tend to be more muscular and physically stronger, they know they can forcibly take what the want. When it comes to sex, therefore, it's understandable that boys go after it. And when they get it, they see it as theirs.

How this translates is that the girl primarily becomes a body. "She's hot!" The boy tries to get her to give him sexual pleasure. Girls equate giving this pleasure as becoming of value to the boy. The boy thinks more in terms of the act. So, when boys have sex, they tend to go fast. Their excitement overrides the intimacy. Their want of immediate gratification is so present, that the human exchange, the vulnerability of the sharing goes unnoticed. The boy, for all his power, misses the truth of the experience. The truth of being so present with another risking human is not on his radar. As a consequence, boys and likely most adult males, as a rule miss out on the self-learning and the deep intimacy that sexual sharing can offer.

Boys copy what they've seen. They've seen males being the masters. They've seen males focused on having orgasms. They've seen females being for the males. Thus, it's imperative for our teenage boys to receive a counter message. In some ways, this is almost an impossible challenge. It means not only confronting our own fears of being open about sexuality and talking frankly about it, but taking on the massive sex industry prevalent in movies, magazines and overt pornography. It flies up against all those adult men's lives that have been spent as copies of the shallow sexual behaviours that they grew up with. Yet, the immensity of such obstacles doesn't mean we can't try to shift the ocean liner one inch at a time. Counsellors and sexual education classes can start asking boys what they want from sexual experience and how they came by that want. They can introduce an exploration of what sexuality is, about what intimacy is, and about how the pornography industry has imprinted on all of us and stolen from us the true nature of sexual intimacy.

It cannot be stated how detrimental pornography is. Not explicit sexual images or video or talk in themselves, but pornography that is intended to captivate and procure a paying audience. If a couple wants to photograph themselves or video themselves having sex for their own stimulation, or even to show it to others, that isn't necessarily a negative. Within our personal realms there are a myriad of personal tastes and proclivities. But the massive preponderance of the explicit visuals available to us are produced by merchants out to captivate and hook customers. The addictiveness of that pornography is cultivated and real.

When we teach our kids about masturbation, it is vital that we teach them not to masturbate to pornography. There are especially negative consequences from masturbating to the explicit videos that flood the internet. This has nothing to do with morality, though there is certainly no harm in that factoring into it. When teens masturbate to pornography, it takes them away from self and attaches them to the sexuality of others. Those others are the exploitive, profit driven sex industry. They design the sexuality in pornography and that artificial sexuality inserts itself into the developing consciousness and developing sexuality of the teen. Thus, inevitably, it takes the developing sexuality into new directions that do not stem from the teen's nature. And it's highly addictive.

Schools need to devote teaching units on pornography. Our teens need to understand how it works, why it exists, who is profiting, who is being victimized, and how they will be affected by it. These units need to be developed carefully, and they need to be hard hitting. Our kids need to be brought into the light about how their developing minds work.

We confuse stimulation with sexual appetites and sexual proclivities. Anyone can find themselves stimulated by explicit sexual depictions. That says something about the power of sexual depiction and our human wiring. It may say something about our background, the external experiences we have had which set us up for stimulation by any specific sexual depiction. *It does not say anything about our own true sexuality or proclivity, that which, we as an identity, were born to have.* But the attachment, the lure, the brain chemistry consequences from viewing and masturbating to pornography created by others, can mask this truth, can fool us into thinking the reaction comes from who we personally are.

The apologists for the sex industry will insist they are only giving people what the want, feeding people's sexual needs. This is a lie and a self-serving distortion of reality. It is on the same continuum as a drug pusher insisting that they only supply the customer with the product that the customer wants, the same continuum as the abuser or rapist who claims that, since the victim didn't resist, it wasn't really rape.

This is all true for human beings of any age, but especially true for developing humans. That's why, instinctively, we have protected children from overt sexuality for centuries. We don't expose them to those practices because they aren't ready for it, have not developed their own identities, or their own sexual identities. Once someone has experiences and has formed into the person they are, the sexual person they are through their own discoveries, then any exposure to pornography has some experienced self, some lived context to bounce off, and there is some deflection. Before that happens, when the child or teen gets into pornography, then what they see becomes their experience, it becomes their context. The external, the other's sexuality, the other's personal motivations, usurp what should be growing from the child. They become the sexual context, become the child's sexuality rather than allowing the sexuality to emerge from within, the way their nature intended.

CAROLINA - Many adults blanch at the idea of giving teens direct sexuality education. They believe it's the domain of the parents to take on this job. To those critics I say, live up to it then. Ensure your kids get the full array of education they need from you - masturbation, orgasms, same sex ponderings, intercourse positions, oral sex, etc. If you can give that to them, then great. If you can't, then let someone else do it. And every parent, regardless of their religious or personal convictions, knows that the vast majority of parents won't do it. So, those that are prepared to offer that education to their kids, don't stand in the way of the education system from reaching out to the rest that won't receive it at home.

Another concern is that these topics are too sensitive, that the teens will feel embarrassed or clam up. Initially there will be some of this. As it becomes accepted as common practice, that will disappear. As even the first lessons progress, that will disappear. Kids who have already experienced sexual intrusion or abuse will be triggered by explicit sex education classes. That's all the more reason to hold them. Those kids will show themselves, one way or the other, which should lead to some counseling intervention, and then their healing can begin.

When we avoid, we leave whatever is there to percolate or fester and we leave other influences to wreak their havoc. Kids are not so hesitant to enter into the nitty-gritty of their sexuality. Carolina, a grade 12 student, came into my office to discuss a troubling habit she had developed. At some time a couple of years before, she had been flicking through television channels on her parents' satellite TV and had come across a sex channel. She had watched. Since then, over the months, she had become driven to tune the shows in on a weekly basis. She had begun masturbating while watching the shows. Now she was worried and no longer wanted to be doing that.

Carolina needed a reality check. Was she a bad person for engaging in such behaviour? In itself the answer is, no. But my job was to see beyond the surface, and hear what she was really saying. There was no way that a 17 year old girl was coming in to see a male counsellor to tell about her sexual behaviour unless she was pretty upset. (The same as shall be apparent with the story of Jasmine which follows.)

Masturbating to a visual depiction of sex is common. Boys have been doing it for centuries. Girls likely not so much so, but only because acting on their inner stimulation has been proscribed throughout history. In secret, much goes on that will never be reported on. In Carolina's case, it was her feeling of compulsion and her feelings of uneasiness that needed attention. I had her go step by step to tell me how and when she had first come across the TV shows. What was going on in her home and in her life at the time. The point is to find out what the contact with the sex movies had latched onto in her psyche. What had they triggered?

We talked about her parents and her prior experiences with sexuality. We talked about how she felt, what went through her mind when she watched the programs. We talked about what happened inside her when she masturbated to them. All of this loosens up the compulsion. It shifts the understanding of it and increases self-awareness. By talking with me in a relaxed and trusting environment, and with the related tones of acceptance, Carolina was gaining a deeper sense of self. The behaviour was being placed into an accurate proportion to the rest of her. In other words, it gave her the insight to see it as just an issue to be resolved rather than "THE ISSUE". Not "I am bad" but there is something I need to shift.

The other important aspect was not to let her confuse masturbation and sexual impulses with what she was doing to the sex programs. This is where it was important to talk about our brains and how pornography can be addicting due to the particular stimulation of the brain's nervous system. Lots of research has been done that shows similar brain activity with alcohol, drug, gambling, and sex addictions. Our brains are always potentially ready to wire themselves to various high intensity or pleasure experiences/stimulants.

Caroline had become somewhat wired to the sex programs. I say somewhat because she was not compelled to them every day and was not always thinking or planning to access them. So, we went through what she wanted for herself, how she could attain that, and what she needed to do in regard to flicking the channels to get to the shows. Much of the work was realigning her sense of values and her guilt and shame.

JASMINE - Jasmine's situation was far more serious. Unlike Carolina, who had gotten into her mild addiction just before the sex sites on the internet were really into full bloom, Jasmine had encountered very problematic content on the internet. She was only fourteen when she had blundered onto a sex site while surfing the web. Jasmine lived with her father. Siblings were grown and gone. Her mother was an alcoholic and had rage problems.

One time after a school social event, I was outside with students as they waited for their parents to come to pick them up. It was winter, and it had been an all day affair plus a sleep-over the night before. Jasmine had gotten involved through the efforts of a kind teacher. She was socially isolated and fairly inept amongst her peers. She struggled in school courses and had a history of moving homes, schools, and towns. This always interfered with her developing lasting or solid peer relationships. Jasmine was a lonely kid.

But this school event had gone well for her. She had been involved with various activities and felt, for this period of time at least, a sense of belonging and fitting in. All the other kids were boisterous and merry outside the school as they waited. Some threw snowballs. There was cavorting and laughter. Jasmine didn't take part, but she watched, and I could see her with a smile on her face. This had been a good time.

One by one the other kids' parents drove up and there were happy greetings as the kid got hugs or help getting sleeping bags and gear into the trunk. Lots of good energy. Jasmine saw all this and smiled. Then it was her turn. An older car drove up. It was her mother. Jasmine waved to indicate where she was and walked over to the car with her stuff. No one got out. Jasmine opened the passenger door and greeted her mother. I was close enough to watch. Her mother did not reply. Instead she looked straight ahead with a deep scowl on her face. Mom was clearly furious at having to come to get her daughter. Jasmine quickly got the message. She shut up and silently opened the back door and put her gear in the back seat. She got in the front and looked straight ahead. They drove off. I could feel the strain and silence in the car as they left. I could see Jasmine's closed-in posture. They would drive to their home in silence. Later, Jasmine relayed to me that her mom had been drinking.

Some other conditions that Jasmine endured with her mother were, as a thirteen year old, having to drive her and her mom home after her mom had passed out, once finding out on a school trip that her mom had somehow accessed her bank account and withdrawn her money, and one day receiving a message at school that her mom was coming to see her at lunch break - only to find out she had come to borrow some money from Jasmine. Her father, on the other hand, really loved his daughter. He would buy her anything. Any school activity or trip, she could always afford to go. But he was a workaholic who was seldom home and had no interpersonal skills with his daughter. So, Jasmine really was isolated.

Thus it was that on surfing the web she came across a fetish site involving babies and toddlers and soiled diapers. I won't go into any more detail. Suffice it to say that Jasmine got addicted to that site and ones like it. She would fantasize about the scenarios and even procure diapers to occasionally wear or to obsess on. She would masturbate to the sites. Jasmine was also a Christian. The church, off and on, had been a bit of a social refuge for her. She felt some acceptance there.

Jasmine and I had worked together on several other issues - her loneliness, her struggles with academics, peer interactions, school activities, past sexual abuse, and difficulties with her mother. This had taken place over a full year. We had a good relationship and had covered much territory. The day she came in to tell me about her problem with the fetish, she began by saying, "There's something else I haven't told you about." Her eyes were especially wide. She was fidgeting. I could see how stressed she was. This wasn't like her at all. Normally she'd be smiling when she came in or in tears. Now she was in front of me with this look of horror on her face. She was having trouble breathing. I immediately asked if something had just occurred. She shook her head not. "It's something else. A secret."

I guessed it had to be an abuse incident that she had been unable to bring up before. I relaxed and settled into my chair. "It's okay, Jasmine. Just talk when you're ready. There's no rush." I waited in silence while Jasmine wrung her hands together and stared at the floor in front of her. Every so often she'd look up at me. We waited for over five minutes like that.

Then she looked up and began to tell me of her problem. She was shaking. She was deeply ashamed.

Needless to say, I was totally shocked. Not because of the issue, though I could hardly have imagined it, but because this fifteen year old girl had the guts to open up such a dark secret on her own volition. No crisis had precipitated the disclosure. There was no need for Jasmine to go there except for her own desire to be free. I was in awe of her courage.

After getting a full picture of her situation, I told Jasmine how proud I was of her and how much respect I felt for her. Despite my long and solid relationship with Jasmine, I knew that I could not be the counsellor to get her through this part. But because of that relationship, I knew I could include her in my reasoning and that she would agree for me to pass her on to someone else.

I explained that I thought the issue was very serious, that she had obviously been emotionally tortured by it for some time and that she was now ready to deal with it and let it go. She had begun the process by opening up to me. I said that, in my opinion, she needed someone with specific expertise in the area she was troubled by, likely a female therapist who could walk with her through the route to resolve her attachment to the fetish sites. She agreed to let me tell her social worker and engage in the search for therapy.

That, of course, set in motion the next problem, unbeknownst to Jasmine. I had to get the social worker to accurately understand the seriousness of Jasmine's plight. Believe it or not, the social worker's first reaction was to laugh. Then I had to get her past the notion that people had different sexual proclivities, that Jasmine had simply found hers. This kind of denseness always galls me. Eventually, I got it across that this young teenage girl had been in anguish about her habit and had overcome a tremendous fear to expose it to me, a male counsellor. That the habit was not a person's sexual fetish, but a terrible psychological intrusion which had embedded itself within a developing person not that far from puberty. That she needed an immediate response to her disclosure and that we needed to find a female therapist experienced in such intrusions. The social worker finally understood, but I had to do all the leg work in finding the therapist.

Sex issues just seem to push all sorts of buttons in adults. The consequence is a truncating or short-circuiting of their full reasoning powers. Sometimes the stumbling block is not the adult's own unresolved sexuality or negative experiences, but the adult's ignorance. We have run from open discourse about sexuality for so many centuries, it is no wonder that we are clueless at any given time.

When I first began working in schools, I was located in a small community with a small high school. Everyone knew each other. One of the brutal local practices was the gang rape of young girls by boys at parties on weekends. Everyone would be drinking and one of the girls would be targeted by some group of boys. They would wait for her to go outside, go for a walk, or leave to walk home. Then they'd follow her, grab her, pull her pants off, and take turns having sex with her. Then they'd laugh and run off. They did not call it a gang rape. They called it a "soup line". The girl had been "soup lined".

This "custom" had been going on for years. I knew of adults in the community who had participated in "soup lines" when they were younger. It was common knowledge in the town that these events occurred. Word got around after the weekend about who had been the latest victim. And we at the school would also find out. BUT WE DID NOTHING other than shake our heads and feel sad for the victim. We did not know any better.

We would observe the girl when she returned to school, usually a couple of days after the weekend. She would routinely be in sort of a daze, seemingly not herself, maybe sadness hinted at in her face. WE DID NOTHING. And we were all intelligent, caring adults. Professionals. Travelled and committed educators. Our society and we had just not yet arrived at full or deep understanding of what such traumas meant for the individual girl, what they meant for the community, and what they meant for the perpetrators. I did talk to two boys one time whom I felt close to and asked if they had ever taken part in a "soup line". Both sheepishly admitted that they had. They were 14 years old. I advised them that such behaviour was intensely hurtful to the girl and intensely wrong. That was it. That was as far as I knew to go. At that time.

It has only been in the past couple of decades that sexual abuse and sexual traumas have really taken their place in our consciousness as the soul destroying events they really are. Societal responses and treatment processes are still undeveloped. We still hesitate to be proactive, still hesitate to secure workable and dynamic healing modules. We have not even begun to look at proactive outreach or treatment of perpetrators. They operate in the murky fringes and are kept outside of our own consciousness. Because we are afraid. Maybe because too many of us have the potential to be perpetrators in some form. And because we have not yet developed sufficient knowledge and awareness of how to respond. We are still ignorant.

In many ways, to be charitable to teachers and those involved in the design of education, ignorance is also a part of why our education approaches are so archaic and rote based. We stick with what we are familiar with because we just don't get it yet. We don't have the intellectual development and awareness to see clearly any viable and necessary alternatives to what we foist on the kids.

ROBERTO - The intrusive and powerful effects of pornography on kids has not been examined. Perhaps we run from that truth because of our own haziness and our own sexual appetites whetted by whatever needs we have developed. Until this internet generation, we have not had to face it. Since it is still new to us, whatever research that has been done is sketchy. With kids, there are many barriers to conducting such research. Many communities and jurisdictions are extremely sensitive about anyone probing into the sexual mores and practices of their youth. It is deemed to be meddling or invasive. Some likely see it as planting ideas. But we don't need extensive research to tell us what ought to be logical. We see how pornography attracts and captures adults. Who could suggest it would not be all the more potent with undeveloped teenagers?

Roberto is an example of how sexually explicit messages can affect a developing mind. I worked with him when the internet was still in its infancy. Rap music was the latest genre. Gangsta rap was becoming popular. Roberto and I worked together on his behaviour in classrooms. He was a sharp young guy. A grade nine, he was a bit hyper in the classroom and could be a handful.

He came into my office one day with his earphones plugged in. He proceeded to lie down on my couch and continue to listen to his music. I thought it out of character. He said he just needed to chill for a while. After a few minutes I became curious about what he was listening to. He took off his earphones and passed them to me.

Now, I have always had a difficult time following the lyrics in any song let alone rap. Roberto was listening to rap. But this rap song was easy to follow. It featured the isolated and slow, calm voice of a female describing how to correctly perform fellatio. A beat was playing in the background. I had never heard anything so blatant in my life. Roberto told me he was listening to the song over and over again.

This wasn't a song where the lyrics were in a rhythm with the music, this was an instructional manual. And accompanied with other more usual gangsta rap songs which denigrate women, objectifying them as "ho's" - one song, particularly, was laughing about a 14 year old preacher's daughter who is having sex with 6 adult males in a car - it was a potent and hypnotic lure for Roberto. It was unmitigated license to think and act in whatever way his urges and tastes arose. I was really scared. My attempts to help him see the destructiveness of what he was about fell on deaf ears. "Hey, chill out, Mr. White. It's all cool. It's just music." Yet, Roberto's eyes were slightly glazed. Somehow the music had put him into an altered state.

I brought the issue up at a staff meeting, wanting the other teachers to understand the music our kids had access to. I couldn't get the same track that Roberto had so I got hold of another song about raping a girl in a car and played that for the teachers. Many had a hard time following the lyrics but they got the drift. Many were shocked, but I could see they'd leave the room not giving it another thought. "Kids will be kids." "It's only music." "What can we do anyway." "Oh well." I was dismayed.

The problem was not in the lyrics as such. Ideas, messages, whispers about doing sexual things to others are commonplace and as old as history. But until these most recent times, they were in the domain of private conversation. They were not broadcast publicly and so legitimized. We kept them to ourselves because we knew they were not acceptable as public fare, as actual behaviour the way we whispered them. A dirty joke was spoken to one's own circle because it was dirty. Gangsta rap changed that. It made dirty into mainstream, it eliminated the boundaries of propriety. It blurred the mores and values that had been a fabric.

Celebrated artists were selling millions of albums that elevated and legitimized rape of children, depersonalized an unchecked sexuality, and celebrated the objectification of women in explicit, graphic depictions. The media treated it as normal and acceptable. The sanctity of artistic expression was trumpeted, and this clouded common sense. The lesson imparted to the young was that anything goes. The violent messages and exhortations also prevalent were seen as the right of an oppressed class to express its reality.

All of this is absurd. During the Rwandan genocide of 1994 in which almost a million innocent men, women, and children were ruthlessly slaughtered in a three month killing spree, a key radio station in Kigali, the country's capital, continuously broadcast hate messages and played violent, hate songs. This served as an accompaniment and lubricant to the killing. The radio station's exhortations served as an instructional and motivational tool to expedite and intensify the tribal tensions and direct them into mindless, lethal actions. Kilometres of bodies floated in the river outside the capital. The broadcasts created a sense of righteousness, a legitimacy, and a permission for the unleashing of mindless barbarism. Victims became other than human, they became other than the same as the perpetrators. The killers included women and children themselves.

The point is that the media and its music played a role in genocide. The point is, that when any media broadcasts and thus legitimizes hurt or violence or hatred, then it plays a role in whatever acts transpire accordingly. Anyone that insists that no role is played ought to ask why college sports always have school fight songs, why marines go into battle with their i-pods blaring, or why the colonial armies had fifes, drums, and bagpipes. What does psyching up mean? Why would power messages not be absorbed and internalized by formative minds? Gangsta rap is not the same as the hate radio in Rwanda, but how can anyone pretend that behaviour is not influenced?

Roberto was listening to power messages. And guess what? A year later I convened a meeting with Roberto's parents, the school principal, and the parents of a 13 year old girl. Why? Through the grapevine I had learned that the 13 year old girl had performed fellatio on Roberto in the boy's washroom during school hours.

Ahh... just innocent, coming of age sexual exploration. Right?

The way I understand the experiences of Carolina, Jasmine, and Roberto is that these are only the instances which came to light. There is nothing about the milieu within which they occurred that suggest in any way that it was our skill or resources that found the only such incidents, but that it was a mere fluke that these came to light, while all the similar ones go undetected, hidden to bear later fruit.

I think I want to be hypnotized sometime, because I keep trying to remember my childhood and I remember next to nothing. I want to go back.

I went driving today and I'm doing well. Hopefully, I'll have my license before December. My road test is in just a little more than a week. (grin, cringe)

I'm becoming increasingly attracted to Ramon. He's as, Myrah puts it, "a personable person." Yet one part of me keeps chattering, "You're just doing this because your lonely and frustrated. You want companionship and warmth and he seems willing to give it to you. Nothing could amount of it though, because your parents will hate him. You know they will." My needs get transferred to their needs. Also, I'm unsure because we seem so different yet I'm still attracted to him. And SFX The big no-no/ shh - the - children - are - listening/ let's - go - do - it baby - please word. I've been close before and I'm afraid that I won't stop myself and then regret it later. ......I"M SO FUCKED.

Felice – 16 years old

Creamy
smooth and
also crunchy
everyone's
desire
If only we could
all each have a
chocolate waterfall
and we wouldn't
need to
want

Vanessa Morrison – 14 years old

Feelings
As fragile as an egg
mine
never yours

Austen Ehlinger – 14 years old

3. Has This Really Happened To My Child?

A secondary outcome of our clumsiness and fear about teaching our kids about real sexuality, is that we permit sexual exploitation and abuse to occur in epidemic proportions. It has been a great blind spot throughout the world. Kids everywhere have been sexually victimized for centuries. Our fear of sex, our confusion about sex, and how it has been connected to power has created a scenario where we have lived in a state of denial. Surely, a fundamental reason why we have never developed better laws to protect children, better treatment programs for victims and perpetrators is due to that confusion. Some Canadians may recall the judgment handed down by a Quebec judge many years ago in which he found an accused guilty of inappropriate sexual conduct but qualified it with the pronouncement that his "victim" a 5-year old girl was not entirely blameless as she was a promiscuous young lady!

Of course, our police, our lawmakers, our judges, our clerics, our leaders despite stellar training or post-graduate education are the same children who have grown up with all the same sexual misconceptions, misinformation, skewed imprinting, and confusion as the rest of us. Stag parties inevitably mean pornography or strippers. Check out the predominance of internet porn sites advertising teen sex. Are those indulging in that obsession with youthful sex and nudity that separate from those who create the rules and enforcement by which we live?

Statistics tell us that 1 in 3 girls are sexually abused by the time they are 18. That is certainly my own experience after counselling teenagers over thirty years. The same statistics claim that 1 in 6 boys are abused.

Yet with these astonishing numbers, there is no concerted treatment response. It's like a collective societal, "oh, well." The adult world is riddled with victims and perpetrators who have never healed, never resolved the traumas suffered as children. It is not a stretch to surmise that, on an unconscious level, there is a reluctance to vigorously pursue any direction that might expose the rawness of our own experiences or fantasies.

Adults have this unfortunate response of insisting that others "handle" what they had to "handle". We clutter our existence with superficial but catchy mantras such as "Get on with it," "Go forward," "Don't dwell on the past," "Forgive and forget." And these bludgeon away the natural desire to ask for and acknowledge the need for help, the need for healing. Just look at how we react to physical traumas. We go to physiotherapists, chiropractors, doctors, acupuncturists and any "ists" we can think of for as long as we need to in order to feel better, to get well. When it comes to the deep traumas of child emotional, physical, and sexual abuse, it's as though they are almost deserved as our birthrights or just the luck of the draw. Life changing and embedded like shrapnel, forever influencing and limiting our joy and capacity for self, these traumas are discounted.

This is not to say that some victims don't get the attention and therapy that they need. It is to say that those are the lucky ones, the ones whose experience has somehow found the right response, the ones who found caring and knowlegeable adults who have the resources to fully treat the injury.

Particularly troublesome is the thrust from those who labour the idea of false memory - that claims of sexual abuse arise from over-zealous therapists and those clients who are overly impressionable. Could a determined therapist plant ideas in a client's head? Quite possibly. Could someone imagine or falsely believe they have been sexually abused? Of course. Delusions are delusions. Does that suggest we should doubt someone when they attest to being sexually violated? Hopefully no more than when someone says their house has been robbed, or that they saw a bear on the side of the road. If they have no house, then we might be inclined to doubt that person. If the road they are referring to is in the middle of a big city, maybe we also feel a tad dubious. But, if the person seems fully lucid, shows no indication of ulterior motivation, and can provide details which ring true both rationally and intuitively, of course we should believe.

I have never had a teenager claim sexual abuse and it turn out to be untrue. For every kid who has disclosed to me about that kind of trauma, I know there are many more too afraid, too unwilling to share that kind of truth. It is too painful, and too overpowering. The norm in the teenage world is to keep certain cards close to the chest. Only special circumstances lead to a teen risking that kind of vulnerability. Being a victim of sexual abuse is a dark secret.

Crises can move someone to open it up. Recurring psychological problems can be a motivation - it hurts too much to keep it a secret any longer. A counsellor's reputation for trustworthiness and caring can draw disclosures as can a classroom that brings up the topic and includes with the discussion, evidence that therapy can heal the trauma. Other kids can provide the support for a child to come forward.

The nature of sexual abuse is that it so unfairly strikes to the very core of the victim that it causes a deep emotional sense of powerlessness. In tandem with that is the conviction of now being dirty, changed, or less than. Shame floods into the victim as they desperately try to maneuver their way into control and explanation of why it could happen to them. Shame means it had something to do with them. It serves as a bit of an antidote to the powerlessness and the intense fear that comes with it. If somehow it was my fault or if it is now my problem then that feels less vulnerable, less at the mercy of others.

Abuse is so insidious that we naturally identify with it as our defense mechanism against the pain and wrongness of it. We choose to carry it as though it is "our" secret. Somehow, despite the fact that someone else caused it, was totally responsible, the truth of it is now ours, and thus we can shove it away, try to forget it. Most of this is unconscious.

This explains why it can be so difficult to treat the damage from sexual abuse. Victims not only fear the memory, not only ache intensely from it, but their defence system clutches onto the notion that it is theirs. So, of course, they are not immediately keen on declaring to a therapist, "Here, take it away from me." Aside from the pain or horror at the actual experience of sexual abuse, which ought never be minimized, the accompanying emotion is the great powerlessness during the experience. When uncle, stepfather, auntie, cousin, baby-sitter, boy next door, et al perpetrate their acts of sexuality on the younger victim, their power to do so is indelibly etched into the psyche of that victim. The helplessness of the victim to defend against it is also indelibly etched.

The genitals are in the centre of the body. They are our privates and we learn at the earliest age that there is something more special about them than any other part of our anatomy. So, when an older person comes into that domain, the alarm, confusion, resistance, and panic is at a max. Obviously, life as we knew it has become out of control. All children need to feel a sense of order and safety in their lives. When that gets broken, something has to take its place. The child, in order to survive and keep growing emotionally (and perhaps to not actually die) needs to replace that sense of order or safety. This happens when the child assumes responsibility. If the terrible things that happen are because of the child, because they are bad or should have known better, or somehow are at fault, then the world is still safe, there is still order. The child can accept his/her own blame because it makes the world less terrible and less out of control.

In this regard, the offending adult is not exposed by the child. There is the fear of repercussions, the fear of not being believed, and the fear of provoking worse retribution. But also there is the resistance to giving up one's own control. **If I say nothing, I can pretend it didn't happen. And maybe it didn't, maybe I only imagined it, maybe it wasn't just as I thought it was.** If I say nothing then it's my secret and no one else will know, no one will see me differently, I can keep all as it was. That feels much better than once again re-stimulating that loss of control from the abuse incident.

In therapy with a sexual abuse victim, it helps for them to know how their childhood psyche worked. It helps for them to understand the crucial role that control plays in connection to the abuse. Inevitably, it comes out that control has become an issue in other parts of the person's life. It's like a grassfire, it spreads. Meticulousness, over-achieving, eating disorders, over-eating, addictions, workaholism, neat freak tendency, shopaholism, and on and on - all are about control. Often, they all stem from an early, overpowering incident or incidents of being out of control.

A drunk knows she is a drunk because she has chosen it. A chronic criminal has chosen to pursue that behaviour. An over-eater, a slob, a neat freak - often choose the role because it gives them a sense of control. It establishes a routine or a character that is from their own decision and of their own making and thus whatever happens because of it only does so because of their choices. I may be obese, but it's me, and I made it happen. I'm in jail and I'm a bad ass but that's me, I made it happen. No one tells me what to do. All is a desperate attempt to retain authority, control over one's own life even in those cases where it seems that the person is fully out of control. Only on the surface is that true. Beneath is the knowledge that they chose it all. In this way, the original experience of horror and pain from being truly out of control is kept at bay. Is responded to. It is all a matter of survival. And it makes perfect sense. To the child still inside.

Thus, it is a fascinating scenario when a teenager chooses to go into the truth of their abuse past. What courage it takes! The teenager is still vulnerable. Bad stuff can still happen. While the adult is usually in a position to actually safeguard themselves, to lead their own life, and could revisit the childhood trauma without objective risk of facing a similar hurt and victimization again, the teenager has not that level of development. Adults need only go through the fear. Teenagers need to go through the fear and face the genuine risks that still surround them. The therapist's job is to be such a caring and trustable support that the client can let go of some of the control that, in the deepest part of their own mind, was necessary for survival. The key is to help the client understand that there is a more effective and appropriate method of control that awaits them. Help them to move from one form, which hinders their healing, health, and happiness to another form of control that affirms their true identity and will function to enhance their life.

Again, with teenagers it isn't so simple. They aren't just clients. That's why so few teenagers come forward to open up their wounds. They are still in the battle zone. On the other hand, they are chronologically so much closer to the trauma experiences. That closeness in time means clearer memories, and less impaction of the side effects. If they have developed depression or an eating disorder or substance issues as a compensation to the abuse, that development has likely not been there so long as to have added significantly more damage to that caused by the original issue. By definition, they still have so much of their lives to go and to make be what they would want in their truest minds. So, when teens can be reached then it bodes well for their futures.

ENID - Enid was a beautiful, out-going grade eleven when I met her. She was an honour roll student, well liked. I remember her sitting in my English class, her long dark hair flowing in curls over her left shoulder as she leaned back to cajole with a friend in the desk behind her. Since I was also the school counsellor, I naturally incorporated themes into the English curriculum that would both play to my strengths but also which I thought would be of maximum practical benefit to my students. I had given the class a short story on suicide to read. Now we were discussing it. I had asked each to write about either a time in their own lives when they had felt suicidal, a suicide incident that they had some personal connection with - someone they knew who contemplated or actually committed suicide, or simply about the stress factors in a teen's life that push someone into suicidal thinking. I emphasized that they should only write about what they were comfortable with.

Enid had chosen to write about her parents and the stress they had caused her, particularly the stress that her father had caused her. She had not been explicit in her writing, rather alluded to incidents that caused her shame, incidents that she knew she couldn't tell anyone about. Her message was that the combination of stress from the behaviours of her parents and the pressure of carrying the shame from incidents had made her think of suicide at times in her life.

In the course of the discussion, I mentioned that the most essential point of dealing with a suicidal person was helping them to recognize that things will change, that all situations can improve; no situations are as hopeless as they may seem, with the possible exception of a terminal illness. Enid calmly put up her hand, and proceeded to tell me that she disagreed, that she knew of situations that can't be improved. Her argument was that while one could change their own feelings, their own choices, one could not always change what was happening around them. She intimated that she knew this from her own experience. And that was how we began a long connection which lasted several years until after she herself had a child.

Enid was at that time living with her mom and her mom's new husband. But, for several years from when she was 6 until 14, she had lived with her father and two older brothers. Her father was a lonely, controlling man. A lawyer, he enjoyed a solid reputation in his community. His wife, Enid's mother, had left the marriage, walked out when Enid was six. She had not taken Enid with her. The pressure of living with her husband and his over-bearing, verbally abusive, and unpredictable ways had finally gotten to her and she ran in desperation to create a new life for herself.

While, the two older boys were fine with staying with their dad, this was devastating for Enid. What did it say about her worth, her well-being, that her mother, the same-sex parent, up and left, abandoning her to a man not deemed safe for an adult woman? Enid was in shock. She told me how she remembered feeling confused and terrified that she would die. Her father had never been particularly close to her, being more of a boy's dad, but once his wife left, the man soon turned to Enid for his emotional support.

He began having Enid sleep in his bed at night. In the course of therapy with her, Enid was never able to determine clearly whether or not this sleeping together had become sexual. She had a vague, fearful sense that sexual actions had taken place, but there were no distinct memories. She remembered feeling appreciative of the warmth, of not being alone, but also cognizant that there was something wrong with it. As she grew older, she had become increasingly uneasy about it, and finally at age 10 had managed to get a separate bed for herself.

All this time and until she left to live with her mother, her father treated her in emotional ways that were similar to those one would share with a wife. He took her along on business outings, to dinners, and transferred his control needs onto Enid. She felt herself to be absolutely under his power. At the same time, her brothers kept going to school, as did she, with a complete semblance that all was fine and normal at home. The boys were certainly not going to question their dad, or worse, betray him the way their mother had. Enid was a child. She had no choice.

As I got to know her more closely after that initial classroom discussion, I learned how she suffered with nervous tension. She had a psoriasis condition, she slept poorly at night, and she felt very detached and uncomfortable in her relationships with boyfriends. Though there had been a few boyfriends after she left her father's home, they had never lasted. Enid had entered into those relationships largely at urgings from her friends and because coupling was the thing to do in her circle of peers. Though she had actually liked one or two of the boys, she was always the one to terminate the relationship, always had felt jittery and unnatural. She showed none of this, and none of her friends or the boys would have detected what was going on inside her.

She also worried about her father, worried that he might hurt himself because he was so alone now, the boys having graduated and gone off into their own lives. She knew he was drinking more than he used to. She felt some guilt, not for leaving him because she knew that had saved her life, but for not continuing any kind of relationship. She knew this hurt him.

Her mother was no help. She discussed her past with Enid's father as though it had only been about her, as though the kids had not been a part of it. She frequently expressed triumph that she had finally left him, had gone on with her life, and found Ron, the good man who treated her with kindness and respect. Neither she nor Enid ever talked together about what life had been like for Enid all the years she lived with her father.

During that time, Enid would see her mom for a weekend visit every second week. There was never any serious discussion about Enid staying longer or eventually coming to live with her mom. When Sunday came, it was a given that she'd return back to the father's home. In Enid's memory, this especially became pronounced once her mom met Ron. She was never asked how her own life was progressing. Neither did the dad ask about the weekend visits. The two worlds had no connection. This intensified the split feeling that Enid felt inside herself. From a therapeutic point of view, it was a classic example of crazy-making. Parallel realities neither of which the child has any power over.

Enid's mother was really into horses, and now they and Ron were the focus of her life. She also became pregnant in the year after Enid eventually moved in. So, it was resoundingly obvious to Enid that even though she lived with her mother and was fully welcome there, any deep emotional bond was out of the question.

That she was even there only came about because one day, seemingly out of the blue, Enid had gotten into a huge argument with her father over staying at a friend's place over night. Enid seldom protested her father's regimen, but this time she had. The father had ordered her to stay in her room the whole weekend and that under no circumstances could she go to her friend's, and that was final. For some reason, this was the triggering event that led Enid to begin her own life's journey. In the middle of the night, she had packed her bags and slipped out the door. She told me how difficult this had been. Incredible fear, doubt, guilt, and shock all overwhelmed her. Yet, within that, she felt a determination and an anger that said this was her time. She was going to her mother's house. She hoped her mother had meant it when she had casually mentioned at various times that Enid could live with her and Ron if she ever chose to. That it was never said with any conviction meant it remained a casual refrain similar to the peck on the cheek at goodbyes. But she had said it, and so Enid was going to take the plunge.

To be fair to her mother, when Enid arrived at dawn she was welcomed in. The mother was mainly focused on whether or not her ex had "done something" to her, but she gave no indication that she didn't want Enid there. Perhaps, it was what she herself needed - something or someone else to help her assume responsibility as a mother.

Enid is a perfect example of a teenager living a double life. On the outside, she was attractive, bright, solidly with a group of peers, and never a problem in the classroom. She drank too much on weekends, which was not uncommon amongst her whole grade, but, other than that, no one would suspect there was another side. Yet, she was wracked with competing emotions.

She hated her father and distrusted him completely. But at the same time, she loved him and worried for his well-being. Didn't want him being lonely. Knew that when she was motherless, he had not hesitated to take up her care. She had never felt unwanted or unvalued in his home.

Her mother, who she had yearned for all those younger years, was finally hers again. She had saved her from her father's bizarre ways. Yet, she was the one who had abandoned her in the first place. And she had no depth of emotion for her even years afterwards. She could show the outer pretense of it, say words that one would say, but never actually feel it in any deep way. Enid could always sense this. She could rationalize that her mother was doing the best she could, but inside she felt distrust and resentment, and a gut-wrenching ache. She knew she had never been wanted enough for it to matter. This inner hurt was immense.

From my own standpoint, I always believed that Enid's dad had likely used her sexually as well as emotionally to meet his needs. She had become his surrogate partner and in that twisted mindset, he would have found it irresistible to not satisfy his sexual wants. But accessing those memories was too much for Enid to do considering the skewed emotional foundation she had to live with. The emotional incest was sufficiently overwhelming.

Today, Enid is a single mom of a teenager. After she graduated from high school, she continued on in her own therapy with a private counselor. She hasn't fully healed even yet, but she's happy and she's an involved, loving mom. Also, she works as a therapist for victims of rape.

We don't really want to know about double lives. It's far more comfortable to hold to the illusion of niceness. She's a nice girl. He's a nice man. They're good people. I remember my own duplicity once when I was walking on the sidewalk with my stepdaughter who was about five years old. She had, in my mind, been unreasonable and I was angry at her. As I walked casually along in full view of any passersby, I was squeezing her hand so hard that I knew it would hurt. She started crying. No one could know that it was I who was causing her pain. What a bastard I was! A cowardly, deceiving bastard who was taking out his anger on a little girl rather than acting like an adult and addressing the issue fairly and directly. I knew it then, but at that moment, my own needs outweighed my decency.

As a school counsellor, I watch the hundreds of parents come to school occasions several times every year. They all come with their public faces on. One man once came up to me at a parent-teacher night, also a teacher but in another school, and nervously initiated that he knew I was counselling his daughter and that he wasn't as bad as she said he was. Then he abruptly turned away to resume his teacher visits.

MARINA - Marina was a grade ten girl who I had noticed in the student centre on different occasions. She was beautiful. And she had an infectious laugh and loud sense of humour. Then, just before the start of second semester, she came in with her stepfather. He was there to help her change courses. They were concerned that she would not be successful at her original choices. He was very assertive. She followed along in his wake and nodded that his analysis was correct. He insisted that she was like him, that she had trouble learning abstract concepts, needed more concrete interactions. Physics would not be appropriate. Nor Principles of Algebra. We changed her timetable.

The next notice I had about her was when the vice-principal mentioned that he had heard from a district employee that the girl was really a screwed up kid. Evidently, she had told people that her step-dad, a good guy who was renowned in the community as a good sports fisherman, had abused her. Sympathy was fully with the step-dad and derision directed at the girl. Two months later, the step-dad had moved to another province and was no longer employed. Surprisingly, a court case was going ahead, and the guy had admitted his guilt. The girl wasn't such a troublemaker after all.

Months later, I started seeing Marina to help her make sense of what she had experienced. She was reluctant. It was embarrassing for her to bring it up. Her instincts were to keep it in the past and not look back. She just wanted to be happy.

Just wanted to be happy. Forget and be happy.

The problem is that those soul-shaking experiences don't let us go forward. They don't let us be happy. No matter how tightly we follow any script for happiness or success that seems to fit us, inside we know we are not who we pretend to be. All future joy and accomplishment is layered over the deeper hurts and shames, the ones inserted when we were not powerful or wise enough or developed enough to prevent them. The damage from those intrusions radiate outwards. Compartmentalizing the pain, walling it off so that we can conduct our lives in control, create new families, all works. We fit in. But we are two. We are not at peace.

Marina trusted enough to tell her story, to feel some of the feelings that were frozen. Phil, her step-dad was a cunning and confident predator. He became fixated on the attractive child in his life. He slowly, consistently worked at cultivating a climate of normalcy for his predation. From the time he first moved in, he made a practice of entering the bathroom to do his business while she was showering. At first, she had protested, but he responded with indignation that it was perfectly normal and that she should not be so uptight. She was nine years old at the time.

In this way, Phil began to undermine Marina's judgment, leading her to be unsure of her own appraisal, began to insert his own standards and impose that as normalcy. Marina might be dressing in her bedroom and Phil would wander in to ask a question or to get something. One time, Marina was angry at an intrusion and yelled at him. Her mother came in to see what the commotion was. Marina was still in her bra. Phil barked at the mother to get out, that they were working something out. Mom submissively did as she was told. Maybe, because she had two younger sons, she was afraid of not having Phil's income and support.

But, for Marina, two huge messages came from that incident. One, if mother doesn't see anything wrong then maybe there isn't. And two, Phil is the boss, and Marina's alone with that. As time went on, the inevitable happened. Phil broke down all of Marina's natural defences and a one-sided "relationship" began, Phil doing what he wanted and Marina letting him.

People are often spurred to doubt the child on these occasions, especially if the child is in their teens. "Well, why didn't you say anything? Why didn't you tell on him?" There is an underlying implication that there was mutuality. That the victim was a willing participant. This is especially pronounced if the victim is sharp in various ways - intelligent, accomplished, vocal, popular, confident. It seems inexplicable to observers that she would not blow the whistle on the perpetrator - if it was the way she portrayed it.

As explained earlier, there are many fears and defence mechanisms, particularly the clinging to a semblance of control, which are responsible for the child's silence. Another equally pivotal factor is the simple element of shame. The victim feels such a deep sense of shame that such activities are occurring. She never sees clearly, (in the case of Marina, how thoroughly she was groomed) how powerless she was to fend off the advances. When there is a subtly to the abuse, when it proceeds in incremental stages, the victim is always wrestling with the prayer that it will stop. Shock from the first experience turns to minimalizing - it wasn't that bad, it was only. Then, it's maybe it won't happen again. But as it continues, the victim feels that they've been dug in too deeply. They are very aware of the issue of credibility. No one will believe me. I should have said something right away. This self-doubt, self-reprimand over inaction and the accompanying shame serve the perpetrator so effectively. They encase the abuse in secrecy. The victim walls herself off.

Similarly, if the first abuse instance happens to be intense and full out, then the shock is so overwhelming that it is natural to seize up. Then as that seizing wears off, the actual fear of bringing it up, the unknown of what that exposure will mean feels overwhelming. On top of all this, the shame. Why didn't I do something? Why didn't I yell? To reveal what happened means to admit to everyone that you are soiled now, that you were too helpless to do anything to stop it; it means answering questions, going into the nitty-gritty of acts that horrified you, to be forever branded as an abused person. Secrecy seems easily a better choice.

Another fact can complicate matters. Children and teens do not understand their own bodies. They don't understand that their genitals can respond to touch no matter the situation. Adult rape victims report having had orgasms during the rape. The facile and uninformed reaction is that "she must have secretly liked it". Of course, that's totally false. A body is a body. Nerve endings are just that. So, when a teen's genitals respond to stimulation from a perpetrator, it causes immense confusion and shame. All the more reason to block it all away. Pretend it didn't happen. Pretend it was someone else's body.

This can be incredibly problematic if there were emotional needs being met as well. A lonely child, a child without sufficient positive attention is a needy child. We all need a clear level of affirmation in our lives. We need to know that we belong, that we are of value, that someone likes us. A child without enough of those experiences cannot help but translate some of what an abuser does as being an affirmation. Enid needed some kind of warmth from a significant adult. She got the twisted warmth her father offered. That was better than nothing. Children can easily die from emotional hypothermia.

Indeed, it has been said that perpetrators can pick out safe prospects for abuse in a playground just by watching how the kids interact with each other. The practised predator knows the non-verbal and behavioural signals that indicate which kids will be easiest to manipulate, easiest to act upon, and most likely to keep quiet. The same applies to teenagers.

It must be categorically stated, however, that the victim is never responsible, is never a part of their own victimization. There is never consensuality, no matter how it might appear, no matter how the victim behaves afterwards. A teenager may lie in the arms of their perpetrator, may return again and again to those arms, but that does not equate to consent, to equality, to willingness. It does not change the criminality of the abuse. The truth of the abuse. And I am not here referring to legalities. The laws throughout jurisdictions are just what they are. They are written and acted upon with all the inconsistencies that appear in every other realm. The wrongness I am referring to is the reality, the fact of it all.

Marina had no choice but to go along with Phil's behaviour. Whatever took place was because of Phil's needs overpowering Marina's capacity to choose. Phil knew what he wanted, he knew what he was doing, and he made it happen. Marina bowed under that greater capacity.

JONAS - A sixteen year old, scholastically advanced male student once collapsed in my arms as he painfully recounted an experience in a public campground of three years prior. He had been camping there with his parents. During his walks around the area, a man had crossed his path on occasion. Each time they had made eye contact, and the man had been friendly. Jonas recalled that there was a certain energy he felt from the man, like the brief eye contacts were somehow more meaningful than they ought to have been. Then, on one walk during a late evening, he had come across the man again. The man began talking to him, and the next thing he knew the guy was stroking his shoulders. Jonas froze. The man went to his knees and began to fellate him. When it was over, the boy returned to his parents' tent, never saying a word to any other human until he told me in my office three years later.

When Jonas told me, he was shaking, his face was flushed, his veins were sticking out, he stuttered. I have never been with any student in so much agony. He was absolutely stricken with a shame that revolted him. It was unfathomable to him that he had let the incident occur. Unfathomable that he had let the man cause him to have an orgasm. He did not know what to think of himself other than that he was scum, the lowest of the low. My job was to reflect back to him an accurate picture of what had really happened.

I asked him if when he went to the campground, he was hoping to meet a man for sex? No. I asked if he thought that maybe the man who had assaulted him had likely gone there intending to find someone? Yes. I asked him if when he had crossed paths with the man, he had felt an attraction? No. In retrospect, did he think that maybe the man was of the opposite view? Yes. Had he ever had anything similar ever occur in his life? No. Did he think that the man likely had experience with such encounters, that he had done similar things before? Yes. After seeing the man several times, did he suspect or hope something sexual would happen, think or hope that any intimacy at all would happen? No. When he bumped into the man that evening, was he surprised? Yes. Did he feel any attraction toward him in any way? No. Did he anticipate the man's behaviour? No. Did he now think that the man was likely waiting for him that evening? Yes.

Jonas was starting to get the picture. He was starting to see that the incident only occurred because the man had made it happen. He had nothing to do with it whatsoever. The next obstacle was reflecting back accurately why he hadn't run away or cried out. For a victim to be free, for them to fully accept their victimization they have to understand their inaction on a deep level, a resonating level, where there is no doubt. Otherwise, there is the tendency to retain that element of control in order to spare oneself the fullness of the horror and the powerlessness. If we can blame ourselves then we retain power, which means protection for the future, which means safety. All a bit convoluted but those are the psychological straws the child's psyche is designed to cling to.

So, how to aid/prod Jonas to recognize he could not cry out or run away? This is difficult. It is made easier if there is a strong trusting relationship with the counsellor. The reason victims, and in this case the boy, don't cry out or run away is because they are in shock. It's like in our dreams when danger is at hand and we find ourselves frozen. Jonas needed an explanation of how shock works, how depending on the circumstances, it doesn't spare anyone, especially not a developing person not yet fully experienced in the world. Jonas let the man do his deeds because he was in shock. It was too much for him. The man hadn't jumped out of a bush and grabbed him, but had advanced slowly, had previously established a familiarity. Jonas, like Marina, was lulled or groomed into not resisting a perpetrator's advances.

The reason that trust with the counsellor is so important in this part is because the victim has to believe that shock works that way. Jonas kind of bought it, but he needed to go a bit further. We got to a stage in the therapy where he came into my office in considerable agitation. He was struggling with the why's and the self-recrimination. He kept repeating how he was a failure, a bad person, stupid, and to blame for what happened. I, naturally, kept quietly insisting that none of that was true. I can see myself to this day, my voice gentle and caring, persistently contradicting what he was feeling. But it didn't seem to be helping. He was in torment. Finally, I got the drift. I needed to listen. So, I started saying, "Yes, yes you were a failure, you were bad and stupid." He began crying deeply. The dam had broken.

What Jonas needed at that moment was for me to walk with him into his pain and self-blame. He needed me with him as he went into the deep feelings of that cesspool of no control. As the crying abated and the session ended, I hugged Jonas and he left my office.

The next day he returned to tell me what had transpired later that evening. For the next several hours, Jonas had felt quite miserable and sad. Then as evening stretched on, inexplicably the sadness had shifted to anger and then rage. The rage was all directed at the man who had shocked him and abused him. Jonas became so enraged that he had gone outside and chopped wood for an hour; with each chop, he threw all his anger at the man.

By going with him on his need to self-blame, to feel those feelings, it had allowed them to dissipate, to release and allowed the truer realization and accompanying feelings to emerge. And so Jonas taught me how to listen not to my own mind, but to the mind of the child.

AMRITA - Amrita was a grade twelve student. She was one of my peer counsellors in her grade eleven year, but had moved to another school. I had counselled her for bulimia and we had a good relationship. So, I wasn't surprised when she turned up one day for a visit.

Some months before, she had been staying over night at her friend's home. Amrita's own parents had basically abandoned her when she was eleven years old and a family friend had taken her in and raised her with her own daughter. So, Amrita knew what it was to be a visitor in someone's home. Anyway, that night in the other friend's home, the two girls were in the basement watching movies. Upstairs the parents were asleep. It was midnight. There was a knock on the door.

To both girls' pleasant surprise, it was Edouardo, a boy who had just graduated. He was a bit drunk, but that didn't matter. He came in to join them with their movies. After another hour, Amrita's friend said she was tired and was going upstairs to bed. Amrita was enjoying the movie so she replied that she would come after the movie ended.

Within minutes, Edouardo had sidled up beside Amrita on the couch. His arm went over her shoulder. Amrita liked Edouardo, had always considered him cool and a nice guy. When he started to kiss her on the neck, she was surprised. But instead of saying anything, she just moved a little away on the couch. She didn't want to offend him.

He came close again and put his hand on her knee. She left the couch and went to lie face down on the carpet, still watching the movie. In a few minutes, Edouardo joined her. Lying beside her, he reached his hand under her abdomen and felt for her crotch. She crossed her legs and said that she didn't want this, that she already had a boyfriend. But he persisted. She froze. Before long, he was having intercourse with her. When he was finished, he got up and left, and she went upstairs to bed.

When she told me the story, the tears were streaming down her eyes. She didn't need me to ask questions or offer feedback. She already knew what had happened. Edouardo had taken her by surprise. She felt trapped in someone else's house. She considered screaming but was afraid of what her friend's parents would think. What her friend would think. She realized her error had been remaining downstairs, but she had liked Edouardo, and had never imagined he was capable of that kind of behaviour. She went limp and let him satisfy himself. And then she was left with the repercussions.

In her diary she wrote, "I was not a person to him, he didn't listen, I was a hole to fuck. It didn't matter to him how he got what he wanted. A friend right? Bullshit. I was so bloody careful to get my point across without making him feel bad….. I was still shaking the next morning"

The next days, she said that she felt in a daze. At school, she avoided Edouardo. When they did meet, he acted as though everything was cool, even joking and flirting with her. She abhorred him. But as the days went on, she became depressed, her bulimia flared up, and she could not concentrate on her schoolwork. Her solution? One day at school, as Edouardo was flirting with her she returned it. They began going together. For the next month, she felt like a split person. One part of her was acting warm and interested in Edouardo - they had sex several more times - and the other part was in inner turmoil and anger. She was fully aware that he had raped her, and now she was his girlfriend. She knew it was a mess.

Edouardo began to miss appointments with her, became less doting. They split up. Shortly afterwards, Amrita came to see me. She had basically figured it all out, she just needed confirmation and support. Being a rape victim and not having any way of reaching out to receive solace meant she had to find another salve. Her guardian wasn't safe for her - if she told the woman who was already a stressed person in her own marriage, maybe she would think that Amrita was too much trouble. The distraction from her bulimic habits took some pressure off, but she had learned too much about bulimia and no longer wanted that outlet which she now recognized as an illness. So, she decided to co-opt her assailant, in her mind to make the rape a courtship initiation; resistance became welcome.

For a short time that had worked. It was mind and soul bending, but it was better than feeling a helpless victim. Luckily for her, and she recognized this herself, Edouardo was a sufficient enough creep that he wasn't about to stay in a relationship. She had become free of it and now wanted to begin the process of healing and regaining her self. As with Jonas, a good part of that would entail self-forgiveness.

An essential part of counselling or supporting someone who has been the victim of sexual intrusion or abuse from an older person when they were a child is to choose language and descriptions carefully. It isn't sexual for the child. This cannot be stated emphatically enough. It is sexual or power based for the older person; they are gratifying their wants, but the child is only a receiver. The child is not a sexual player in the interaction NO MATTER HOW IT MAY APPEAR.

Because of this, I always speak with anatomical accuracy. He put his penis in your mouth as opposed to going down or had sex with him. A child doesn't have sex. A teen being exploited by a more powerful person is not having sex. It's important to establish that distinction because it's the truth. Healing is aided by understanding the difference between actions involving the genitals and sexually motivated actions. I help the teen with this by posing such a question: "Did you look at Phil and say 'Boy I'd like to have sex with him.'" If they say no, then I clarify that what took place was not sexual because sexual has the hidden implication of having thought that way. In other words, it is not the child's genital needs that pulled them into the interaction. So, when it is referred to we ought never to describe it as sex or sex acts.

And in this regard, my practice with the healing is to help the victim recount with as much detail as possible exactly what happened. I liken it to slowing down a movie film, slowing it down frame-by-frame in order to see exactly what took place and to recapture the feelings that went with it. Thus, I'll ask about what his penis looked like or where precisely he put his hand when he put it down the victim's pants. I'll want the victim to say, "my vagina". I'll even ask if fingers went inside. This might sound too harsh, making us blanch at the explicitness, but my reasoning is that whatever took place was not the doing of the victim, but it has been sealed into the victim. I want it out. I want it released and allowed to fade away, not to remain buried, walled up as though it was a terrible secret that needed to be guarded or feared. The abuse was not the doing of the victim. Someone else forced it to happen and the shame must not be taken on as though the victim bore some responsibility. So, detail by detail I want it out. I don't want to risk any details remaining kept secret and staying inside as though they belonged there.

The abuse does not belong inside the victim. It needs to be given back to the perpetrator. That's a reason I also ask if by any chance the victim had an orgasm when the interaction occurred. Having an orgasm tricks the victim into self-blame, into the false assumption of participation or approval. If a victim had an orgasm during the interaction and it doesn't come out then chances are high that it's because of shame or fear. By keeping it hidden it stays inside and any other healing or resolution gets layered over top of that secret - that shame based secret, that "it was my fault, I'm guilty, I responded, I must have liked it" secret. And that kept secret can only cause limits later on. It continues the internal carrying of the perpetrator.

Stacey Malysh – 16 years old *(See page 130 Colour Insert)*

RAMONA - Ramona was left at home with Pete, her mom's boyfriend, for two weeks while mom went off to training in a far away city. Ramona was a grade 12 student. One evening, she had to go to pick Pete up after his shift work at the local ice arena where he worked. They were driving out of the parking lot when Pete asked her to pull off on a side road. She did so. Pete began kissing her and fondling her, telling her he was so lonely and had always found her attractive. When he stopped, he apologized and asked her not to tell her mother, that it might cause them to break up and that he didn't want that to happen.

A few days later, Ramona came in to tell me. Actually, she wrote it all out and came in to ask me to read it because it was too embarrassing for her to actually say it out loud. I spent a couple of sessions with her and was able to convince her that she needed to tell her mother about it. When her mother returned home, I phoned her and asked her to come to the school for a meeting. Ramona and I told her together. In shock, her mother broke down into tears. Ramona was in tears. They left arm in arm with mom vowing to settle things with her boyfriend.

Two weeks later, Ramona came back to my office. She was a mess. Indeed, her mom had exploded at Pete and sent him packing. Ramona had felt vindicated and loved. Then, a few days afterwards, Pete had phoned her mother and the two had begun meeting. Just yesterday, Pete had moved back in. Her mother had informed her that everyone makes mistakes and that she loved Pete and Ramona would just have to accept her choice or else find another place to live. She had added that Pete had explained some other parts of the story, which Ramona had left out.

I phoned Ramona's mom and requested another meeting. While I knew that it was not my place to tell a parent how to run her life, I felt that I owed it to Ramona to at least tell it the way it was. We sat uncomfortably in my office. The mother was leaning forward in her seat ready to assert her point of view. She explained that she had thought more about the whole event and that Ramona was not so innocent. "She's an experienced girl, you know. It's not like this is any new thing for her. Ramona is very mature, and Pete wasn't fully to blame." I wasn't about to challenge her about Ramona's past sexual history. Ramona hardly needed that. She sat silently in the corner of my office.

Instead, I looked the mom directly in the eyes and stated, "You are Ramona's mother. Of course, you can decide whatever you want, but that doesn't mean it's right. Ramona was strictly the victim in this situation. Her past experience had nothing to do with it. It was all Pete's doing, and now she needs her mother to stand up and fully acknowledge that. She needs you to stand beside her on this, not beside Pete."

Mom looked back at me and declared that she had made her decision. "Life isn't perfect and neither are people. Pete said it will never happen again. There has never been a problem before this. And Ramona is not always so easy to live with. She's my daughter and she's welcome to live in my home. But so is Pete."

And that was that. I responded the only way I could - "Well, that's your choice. But I believe you are selling out your daughter."

My only consolation was that, in front of her mother, Ramona had heard another adult state loud and unequivocally that she was not at fault. If that had not occurred, there would have been no counter view from the reality being established and ingrained from her mother. Hopefully when Ramona has her own teenage daughters she will come through for them in their times of need.

When I got into the car (the back seat) and didn't see Marla and Linda my first thought was that we were obviously going to where they were. I didn't think they were still sleeping. Two of the guys were in the back seat with me and the third guy was driving. I asked where Marla was and when they didn't answer I got a little nervous. One guy started unzipping my pants and the other guy put his hands up my shirt. I kept shoving the hands out of my pants but whoever this guy was just got more forceful. I never really said anything at the very beginning because I was embarrassed and I wanted to pretend I didn't really notice or something stupid. But when they got more forceful I told them I wanted to get out but the driver kind of laughed. The next part is kind of a blur but when I was tossed out of the car and my shirt was thrown out after me I was extremely out of control. I QUICKLY put my shirt on and ran silently crying back to Marla's house. I layed on my bed after I made sure Marla and Linda were really asleep. I didn't sleep. The next morning Marla and Linda asked if they came back because they thought they heard something. I told them that they did come back but I told them to leave and they did. That morning I found two hickies on my boobs and it was agony going to the bathroom for the next week because of one of the guy's big fingers or hands or whatever was getting pretty violent down in my private area. Nobody raped me. I know that for sure. It was just scary. I never told anyone because of my fear of it being my fault of going into the car. But it was my stupidity that caused it. People would think of me as a slut if they knew.

I considered telling Marla about it for a while but when I found out she got raped then I decided never to tell because I didn't want her to think I was upset about it. If she thought I was upset about that then she'd think I was selfish for thinking of myself rather than her who really did have something significant happen. This thing that happened to me doesn't really matter. I have never thought about it since it happened. Maybe that's "blocking it out" but I don't have the right to have it as a memory.

This gross, disgusting, repulsive body that I would do anything to have the courage to get out of.

Another Blocked out memory, that I remembered.

When I was about 10 we used to visit my Aunt + Uncle in Penticton a lot. My cousin was about 16 then. He was a big brother to me when I was really young but I started to notice that he treated me different when I was 10 or 11. When my parents and Aunt + Uncle went out to walk the dogs he'd ask me to come lay down on his bed or on my bed with him. I liked him a lot because he was always my friend. I trusted him. He'd take off his clothes and

*lay naked under the covers. Then he'd grab my hands and pull me near him.
Once again I pretended to my cousin and to myself that I didn't really know
what was going on but I really did know. Now when I look back I realize
that. If I was hesitant to touch his penis then he'd get the cat and put it doen
there and then tell me to pet the cat. When I would pet the cat he would take
my hand and make me touch his penis. I thought at the time that it tickled
him because that's why he kind of "groaned and laughed slowly" but now I
know he was making me give him a hand job. When my hand was wet after
I thought it was just sweat. Maybe I didn't really think it was sweat but I
pretended it was sweat. One time he put my head down by his penis but I
giggled like I didn't understand and pulled my head up. But he got mad at
me and told me I was being mean. I didn't want to be mean to him because I
thought he was a good guy so I put my head under the covers and shut my eyes
and waited until he was done. It was very gross and after that I hated him.
When he came near me after that with his grin on his face to take me downstairs I'd run away as often as I could. But still sometimes I'd have no escape.
I stopped thinking about it and did it mindlessly. Blindly and mindlessly.*

*This gross, disgusting, repulsive body that I would do anything to have the
courage to get out of.*

*So, my few sexual encounters haven't been positive - My cousin, Bob, the
guys in the car. When you asked what the penis meant in the picture I didn't
really know what it meant. But when I draw to express myself things come
down on the paper that I sometimes don't realize what they mean. That penis
was a hatred of mine and I didn't really take the time to think about why I
hate it. Now, looking ar sex in my past I see why I hate my body. well actually, I hate my body half for those reasons and half because it keeps me here.
When I'm alone and the silence and the sounds lock me into my thoughts
I truly feel deep down that this physical life is pointless and hateful. Sex is
simply a pleasure to the physical life, therefore I hate it. Now sadness is on me
and the tree on the wall looks like me. The fading roots and dead branches.
When I look at that tree I see myself. That's why I loved it so much. Why are
my curtains always closed? And the door always shut? And the lights always
off? The answers cannot be from my physical life. My dark angel that carries
me under his black wing guides me and grants to me darkness. Darkness is
good. In the dark, alone with music. My eternity now and after. Good-bye
cruel world.*

*Cruel WORLD . Look what it makes me. Look what the yellow terrible
sun does to me. I am a black raging sun and nobody should love me. I hate
more than I love. I must belong to blackness and darkness. My show that lasts*

for as long as I live. Where's the point? Where's the reason? Where's the bridge to throw my body away? Where's the razor to let myself decay? Why don't we all die? This eternity of slowly dying. When will it end?

God Fucking Dammit

THIS SUCKS

FUCK THIS

Crazy. Crazy Crazy I must be crazy I can't see through this blurry vision. These tears that won't fall. Tear stained eyes but dry cheeks. Existentialism Existentialistic. Build a wall to surround me and to cover me, keep me safe from myself keep me safe from everyone else. They'll hurt me. I'll hurt them. They'll hurt themselves.

This black cloud that cradles my mind. My poor, poor corrosive mind. Beating me down

making things hard. too hard. Future? What? FUTURE?

What future? What future is there for a self-destructing animal? My gross body. I'd like to be free. I'd like to have the freedom of being. To fly, to have somewhere to fly to. Maybe dying would cure me. Maybe death would quench the ache in my stomach. My knowledge I've forgotten. Tear by tear that swell then dry. The bleak present. The bleak future. The _____ past? What's my past? They say they love me. How can I be that sad. They've trapped me with good intent. where did my evil come from? The evil came when I began to think. I should be ignorant.

Existentialism   Existentialistic

We're all alone. we are born alone and we die alone. We live alone. Each seeing this place differently each knowing a different story with a different tune. Scream if you like, laugh if you like. Yell a bit maybe even a little silence. But nobody will hear you. You are alone in your sound. Try to share but you can't escape yourself. There's hope for when you die. There's a little hope. The urge to be truly free scares me but time has shown me that my urge only escalates. Up and up and more and more. My desire. but this is strange tonight. I am having after thoughts. Something new is yelling so loudly that even my dark state isn't all bad? It's not all bad?

Oh Fuck The two opposites always clashing clashing

The day/ the night

The sun/ the moon

Amy – 16 years old

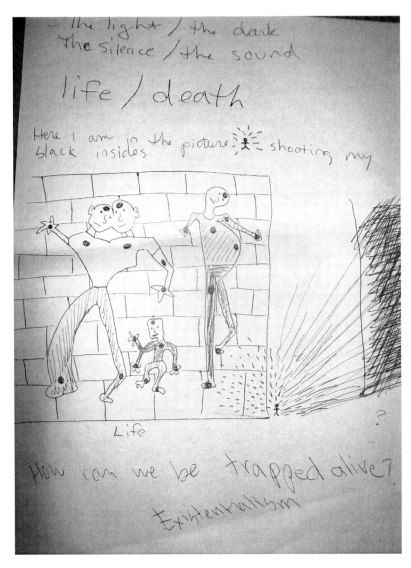

Amy – 16 years old

4. Whatever It Takes

In my office, I have the walls covered with a wide collection of art and objects. Some mementos given to me by students, grad photos of others, photos of my own kids, drawings by them, framed pictures, a boxing poster - HITMAN HEARNS VS SUGAR RAY LEONARD, a laminated newspaper page from 1958, a blue stained glass hummingbird, a rubber rat atop my computer, a Mao hat on the rat, and most of all I have clutter, clutter on my desk, on the floor. It all reflects my various tastes. And it's also by design. When kids are in my office, I want them to find it interesting. I want them to be signaled that I'm different. And with the clutter, I want them to be modeling looseness, imperfection, ordinariness. That it's okay. Maybe some kids are taken aback a bit, but that's good too.

Sometimes, I drive kids in my car. That too is messy, undusted. I'll have a coffee cup on the floor. It likely makes some cringe a bit. I'm glad, because again it sends a message. We're all human. Authorities are human, flawed, and all different.

That coordinates with one of the messages I imply with my counselling - sometimes, I don't have answers, there are no solutions that can make it all better. A totally clean, organized, orderly, polished environment or teacher's desk/classroom signals that life can be that way - we can make it exactly the way we want it, other people's lives are orderly, organized, spotless, perfect. My message is that no, there is no spotless life. We're all broken in different ways. I think that message, that model, helps people relax a bit, go easier on themselves maybe, see the world more accurately, and give themselves space to figure things out, understand, rather than build walls or false self-images. Or maybe it just helps them feel better than me, that at least they're not as messy as me, have higher standards. That's good too.

Another practice I have is that I keep my office windows covered. I choose the privacy. If a kid is going to speak of their deepest experiences and feelings, perhaps breaking down, I don't want that for public view. Many advisors insist that it is dangerous to have that seclusion - they warn that a kid can make accusations. Leave the door open a crack even; protect yourself.

I've never looked at it that way. I don't see kids as potential threats. I see them as children. From my standpoint, the only reason a child opens up is because they need to and for that moment they trust me enough. Sure, there are kids who, having been terribly hurt and still suffering that emotional damage, could possibly manufacture an accusation. They'd do it for attention or to punish an adult, an authority. But those kids are usually easily discernible. They seldom go very far with me. Those types of defence mechanisms tend to make them too walled away from the real palm in their souls that they don't enter my domain for long. I've never felt uneasy or vulnerable in my counselling office with a child, and there have been so many raw, exposed interactions.

I've had teenage girls and boys come with me to a more private location where they could scream. Obviously, staying in the office or near the school wouldn't allow for screaming. Being too near residences in general precludes that kind of release.

AMY - One particularly interesting time was in the forest on a nearby low mountain. I drove Amy there, asked her to walk along a path by herself while I waited at the car. I asked her to run and scream. We had gotten to a part in her therapy where she was telling me about being forced into giving oral sex to her older cousin while on extended family get-togethers when she was nine. As a teen later, she had been raped by a "boyfriend". Though a brilliant artist and a top student, she was quite emotionally unstable. As a sixteen year old she could not stand being in school, felt distant from most of her peers, except for another friend who had also been raped and who was dabbling in cocaine.

I saw her situation as precarious. We had a lengthy connection and had covered lots of territory. I wanted her to have privacy. My view is that the natural world has a healing aspect. It can allow different parts of ourselves to show themselves. It is an accepting space. The flora and the pulse of the fauna, the earth itself are accepting. One feels relaxed and more peaceful in nature. Usually. So, I judged that such a setting would be easiest for Amy to access some deeper feelings. She would not feel any uneasiness from being in a confined space. She could stretch with the expression of the emotion. That's why I had her run as well. That involves the body. Loosening it. Activating its capacity for flight and, as such, its power. That was something she could not have done when she was being victimized by the cousin or by her boyfriend. She could not run. She could not scream.

Knowing I was behind her, had come with her, understood her, provided safety and confidence. So she ran and screamed. She was already an artist. This was just extension. After she finished and had walked back to the car, we sat in the late afternoon sun and talked about what the experience was like. I held her afterwards, and then we drove back to school.

All of this was a risk. Her parents did not know. The school did not know. I would not ordinarily take such a risk. Ordinarily, the kids I counsel would not have been ready nor would they fit such a risk. I'm not stupid nor a risk taker. I like safety. On the other hand, I do prioritize the well-being of the children I see. I had to trust my own judgments. And whenever I'm uncertain, I confer with a colleague.

An effective counselling relationship is all about trust, building trust. That happens as each step of the interactions occur. Each level of trust can only be achieved as time and the shared story evolves.

Amy needed me to go that far with her. She needed to go out there. It is ludicrous to accept one's pain and confusion as just the way it is, something to be tolerated or lived with. She was a child still developing. She deserved to release the terrible experiences she had been forced into so she could resume her own birth-given self's journey. That's really what healing is all about, really what therapy is all about. It's getting the client back onto their own path, the one they would have followed if others with more power hadn't interfered and imposed their own needs on them when they were too vulnerable, too undeveloped to fend those impositions off in a healthy, workable way that would leave their own development intact.

The past cannot be undone, but the effects of the past can be corrected. And like learning languages, it's easier when it can be done at a young age, as close to the damaging experiences as possible. So, in my opinion, it was appropriate to go that distance with Amy. It's always opinion and judgment. There are no guarantees. No one knows. We just think we do. I pay intense attention to how the child I counsel is reacting. I use those observations to tell me which direction to go, which questions to ask, which exercises to try.

When I first told Amy what I had in mind, I watched and listened - all her body reactions, what she said, how she said it, the tension or lack of surrounding it. As we drove to the mountain, about 15 minutes from the school, I kept my senses alert. How was she relating to this foray? Did she seem okay with it? Did she understand? Or was she just following my lead because I was the authority and I had her trust? Just because we set out to do it did not mean we couldn't change direction and return to the school.

The whole point is to find and to fit what will work for the client. A salient aspect to my therapy style is to always keep the kid in the loop. I don't spring things on them. I explain the reasoning: explain where I'm coming from. I want them to understand how our emotional and survival structures work. I see this as including them in their own healing. I emphasize from the start that we will walk together, that there are two of us. That they need me for support and feedback, for me to pay attention, and for my experience. I need them to know where to go, to understand the exact reality they experienced, and to show me what is helpful. Together we go on a journey of truth. A journey of health. A journey of completeness. That is the plan.

It empowers the client to always be explaining what I'm doing and why and how I use the phrasing I do. Not in excessive detail but whenever it seems likely the client would wonder or needs to understand the process in order to better understand how any particular habit or reaction within had developed. That understanding is imperative. It's not like going to a surgeon and having an operation. The patient only needs the problem fixed. In therapy, the client needs to be actively aware and participate in the fixing. When it really comes down to it, as crucial as the therapist is, the only way resolution, release, and healing comes about is if the client wants it and is willing to set out the map for the therapist to follow. That's why the key parts are trust and relationship. The whole point is to get to where the client needs to go, and thus it is not the therapist's own maps that are crucial.

In Amy's case, it produced an unexpected benefit only a month later. I got a phone call at 11 P.M. from a school colleague who knew I had a counselling connection with Amy. In that instance, Amy was at another male student's home, she was high on drugs, and her father had been called and was there and in an agitated state. I went immediately.

When I arrived, there was Amy's dad, Fred arguing with his daughter and insisting she come with him. The boy, a sort of boyfriend, was standing back and looking fawningly at Amy as though to say she should stay with him at his house. Amy was coherent but not herself. The boy's dad was also there, and Fred was ready to blame everything on him, alternating between trying to reason with Amy and gritting his teeth in an almost physical challenge to the other man.

I went to Amy and gave her a hug. Then I took her aside and spoke calmly, the same way I would if she had come in to my office to see me. I wasn't going to be part of the drama or the alarm. Kids use drugs. I wanted to know which ones she had used. Her eyes told me that her mind was quite off, she was not inside herself. I suggested that she and her father go with me to the home of the man who phoned me, whose daughter was also Amy's friend. Everyone agreed and off we went.

I wanted to shift the setting, defuse the emotionality, and get a clearer sense of where Amy was at, what was happening inside her at the moment. In the other home, we all sat and had tea. I asked some questions and basically tried to attain a level of calmness inside Fred so that Amy would not be so oppositional to him. I also wanted to ascertain how much Amy could sustain attention, coherence, and a sense of presence. I needed to know who she was and what she was capable of while under the effects of the drugs.

After a half hour, I decided that I was not comfortable with Amy simply going home. I suggested that Fred drive her to the hospital sixteen miles away and have her stay over night. I felt uncertain as to her stability. To me, it felt as though she could get lost further, could run away from home once she got there and end up doing more drugs, or worse, could do something to harm herself. It wasn't worth the risk. In spite of her impairment, Amy agreed to go to the hospital.

As much as I'm willing to take risks and go outside the box with therapy, I always err on the side of caution when I'm not sure of someone's mental state. Fred did not want to have his daughter go to the hospital. Amy did not want to go. The hospital might not have wanted her. Everyone might have thought that the mental health counsellor had over-reacted. That was fine with me. I knew that I was maximizing the chances that Amy would be safe.

She was admitted later that night. Certainly I think it transpired the way it did because I had reached a level of relationship and trust with Amy, which let her accept my feedback that the hospital was the right place at that time.

Amy and I had another rather unique aspect to our therapy connection that involved a certain risk on my part. She was troubled by recurring nightmares. They would wake her up in the middle of the night and leave her deeply upset. Obviously they were related to the abuse I mentioned before and to other painful events that had taken place. My suggestion was for her to phone me as soon as she was shocked out of her sleep by the nightmare. I slept with a phone by my bed.

Twice I had 2 A.M. calls. Each time I would have her tell me about the nightmare, detail by detail. Ask her what it made her feel. See if there were any connections to actual life. It was like talking someone into reality again. As the minutes would pass, I would hear her voice relaxing and hear her becoming sleepy. And then we'd hang up and both go back to sleep. The point was to reach into her inner world and join it to the actual outer world. Because I was real and my voice was attentive, caring, and calm, she could fix onto that. She could integrate what she was feeling, what was being triggered, with the present.

The nightmares stopped.

Again, many would shake their heads at this kind of closeness with a client, let alone a teenager. There would be concerns about enmeshment and lack of boundaries and care taking. My response is that each of those are legitimate concerns. I'd have them also if I heard about a counsellor going so far outside the norms. But I'd also want to hear where the counsellor was coming from, what else was forming the basis of that client relationship, and most importantly how common was such a practice. Was it happening with other clients? If it happens often or as a rule then I think it suggests the counsellor is meeting his/her own needs.

Counsellors, doctors, teachers, any people with access to the intimate parts of other humans can easily get lost in that intimacy. We all have needs, some we are conscious of and others that are unconscious. I always check myself. Amy was a special situation. We had walked a ways together. Her need was great. Everything we did was limited by time in that I knew she would be graduating, and we had these short few months to do this work. Most importantly, and as I mentioned earlier, I am always upfront with every step I take. When it's outside the norm, I talk about it. I talk about boundaries. I make sure the client knows what and why, and feels free to say no or to alter any step. It's all about bringing the client into healthy, active control.

I often wonder if part of the fear about closeness with teenagers is because of the haziness that exists between teen and adult sexuality. We live in an over-sexualized world in which sex is a constant and ubiquitous commodity, marketed at every opportunity, sometimes accompanied by red faces or simple wink-winks. Adults live with much confusion over sexuality boundaries. Thus, the minefield that our kids are born into.

In my over 20 years as a high school counsellor, I have never had a sexual thought about a student, never felt stimulated no matter how physically developed the teenager was. Teenage girls with cleavage showing, with the top part of their butt cracks showing, with a sexual aura to them - none have ever triggered in me any sexual response. I look directly into those young faces and young eyes and see only children. Sometimes I embrace them, even hold them for many minutes during therapy if they're in distress and it feels appropriate. I have looked into those young eyes and heard their stories in an intimate way. I have seen, experienced, who they really are. They are children. This pulses off them as blatantly as bright sunshine.

They think, see themselves, see life, undergo emotions, and daydream as children. Grade 12 students all gussied up and ready to graduate are still children. They are young, naive, unaware of life, unexposed. Those who have been victims of the worst scenarios, those emotionally abandoned to parent their own parents, those actually living on their own - they all are still kids inside. That's why adults ought not ascribe any sexual persona to teens. Their insides are who they really are. Most teachers and other adults as a matter of course are, too often, only in contact with the outside.

They look at the flesh in front of them and react according to how that flesh fits their own tastes and needs.

In truth, I think that teens would be relatively quick to sense ulterior motives or ulterior thoughts if a counsellor had them. I talk to many of my clients about this very topic. Because they become so intimate with me, so trusting, I talk about boundaries and how their trust for me must not give them a false sense about all adults or authorities. I try to work with them on developing their own senses, trusting and paying attention to their intuition, picking up signals.

So in the past when administrators have expressed cautions about my covered windows I suggest they talk to some of the kids I see. Ask the kids.

Ellen – 14 years old *(See page 131 Colour Insert)*

Help
A furry little stuffed
animal can help you
through your problems
better then some people
and they don't even
move

Rohindra – 13 years old

5. Factories Or Schools - Teachers Or Bosses

Teachers like their authority. In some ways, we are like policemen. We are attracted to the job because in our small classrooms, we are the law. We get to say how it is. Power. Once the doors are closed, teachers can say and behave whatever way they want to. They are usually bigger; they have better language tools, have the threat of marks, and can spin the reality any way that suits them. Plus, they can call on an administrator to back them up if a kid causes them a problem.

In schools, the odds are stacked against the kids. I have little experience in grade schools, so every time I refer to schools and kids I'm essentially only talking about schools of grades 8 to 12. There might be much overlap with the younger schools but I don't have the background or expertise to speak to it.

I telephoned one of my superiors in the school board office recently to release some bile. It was somewhat unprofessional in that it came close to breaking our teacher code of ethics. I told him that our schools were too often dead zones. They were not about learning but about maintaining orderliness. And though this conversation was about our particular district, I know for a fact that the criticisms apply to schools in general.

Before going any further, I need to qualify my critique. Of course, there are exceptions. There are schools everywhere that are vibrant, thriving, and meaningful. There are teachers who bring exceptional energy and talent to their classrooms. There is stimulation. Deep and very lasting learning does take place. But none of this is the norm.

The norm is that schools are wholly dependent on individual teachers and individual programs that they house. An excited teacher with commitment and sharp skills can make a classroom hum. Programs that are tailored to involve full spectrum learning, that are focused on the needs of the students make a school hum. This is why in any particular school it's easy to see where the energy lies and where it doesn't.

Sports programs are at the top of the list. Teachers coach because it excites them, because they get personal highs from it. Thus, they put their full energy into it. Kids choose sports. It's voluntary, so they are open to learning, improving, open to the notion of success. There is excitement, joy and full involvement.

Then there are fine arts programs. Again, the kids choose these courses. Because of the creative aspect, teachers often feel less pressure to achieve marks from their students. It is this creativity which draws the teacher and students together. It offers a chance for them to have fun together, to share in a common passion or at least common interest. Kids choose fine arts because they like it not because they have to. Not surprisingly, those that end up in an art class because there is nothing else to choose often get in the teacher's bad books. Clashes become considerably more prevalent than with those students who are into the art.

A dance program at a school I was in had a huge sign-up every year. The teacher could not offer enough blocks to fit all the kids in. Twice a year she would hold community attended dance galas. It was always standing room only. Hundreds of dollars were spent renting costumes. The galas were rich spectacles of movement and theatrics. It was high quality, and everyone who attended left feeling in awe that the dancers were just kids and that this was just a school production.

What drew the kids to that program were two key components. First, dance is creative, it's physical, and it offers freedom. The second was that the kids knew they were going to get good at it, they could see the excellence in the outcome. They wanted that kind of achievement, and the stage that went with it. The boys who signed up, instead of being derided as "fags" were quietly respected and envied. There wasn't one male in the school who didn't wish they could be out there on the stage so involved and so unabashedly showing their stuff. But most were too afraid to go for it.

The teacher was totally into the whole scene. She wanted the kids to get good at dance. She aimed for top quality and transmitted that expectation to the students. She mentored and groomed some to choreograph their own numbers for the productions. The teacher didn't see herself as the star; she saw the outcome as the star. Satisfaction came from the heights the students got to.

This combination of teacher expertise, expectations and personal warmth and involvement with her students made the program special. It sets the template for what education and schools can be and should aim to be. When all those students hit their sixties they'll still have vivid memories of their dance classes. They won't remember a thing about their academics other than what personalities they liked and hated. If that.

Academics in schools are the broken part. They are the dead part. In this century, communication, knowledge, discovery, and virtually every iota of the intellect has been expanded and altered. Academics and how we teach them remains the way it was in the 1950's. Teachers are not trained professionals in the way one presumes from that terminology. Doctors might be trained professionals. For the most part teachers are people who have gone through university and learned subject matter. They then come into a classroom and regurgitate subject matter. This regurgitation takes the form that best fits the comfort zone of the teacher.

Teachers are trained in how to compose and enunciate instructions. How to lay out a sequence of units to have the students cover. That is not teaching and it certainly is not about learning. Teachers might be taught about how to manage student behaviour in a classroom. Again, that has nothing to do with teaching or learning, it's all about keeping order and quiet so instructions can be heard and so other students can have quiet to do their assignments. Teachers may learn how to organize, how to set up group activities, and how to develop effective tests all with the intent of achieving their goals.

Our schools are about assignment giving and assignment marking. They are not about thinking. They are not about developing minds. Teachers do not learn how to bring about either of these. We hope that it will happen. We hope that by giving all the assignments and forcing the students to read all the information that intelligence will grow. Just hope.

A colleague of mine has long insisted that kids learn in spite of what we do as teachers. He'd examine kids' scores on reading and achievement tests and see little correlation between teaching styles that were current in the school.

Kids are failed daily by our education system because it's built on lies and deception. The number one priority is to ensure a comfortable and predictable workplace. We write and talk a good show but the actual workings within schools tends to be flat and bankrupt. Again, I'm not talking about fine arts or sports programs or some other electives. I'm talking about the academics, supposedly the core purpose of a school. Parents believe that their kids are in school to learn, that learning of the highest caliber is occurring. Administrators and teachers try to claim it is, and when it isn't they blame it on the students or parents. They seldom look at themselves.

All direction comes from the various departments of education. They too are, often, out of touch. Their mandate is to justify their existence. To talk the latest talk. What actually transpires on the ground in the classrooms is so far from their purview or concern. It's been stated that the teacher which school superintendents most desire is the teacher that once hired is never heard about again. They obviously don't want to hear anything negative because that trails back to them, and they'd have to do something about it. They also don't want to hear anything really good. That puts pressure on the rest of the system. That also gets people's attention. Gets people thinking and wondering about what's going on. And a teacher that comes into the limelight might later make demands in some way. More funding for a project. Maybe expect to develop something more innovative that threatens the equilibrium. Or simply cast colleagues in a lesser light.

School administrations and education departments are all about keeping things level. No attention is good attention. Let it all just be a machine that hums along. No scrutiny, no parental or media attention. Then each can relax and feel comfortable. This is especially the case as personnel age.

Often, the best teachers are the newest and youngest ones. Not all of them. Some come in with such restricted world and self-views that they simply put their youthful energies into restricting the kids, into asserting their power. And they're not as good at that as the veterans who've been doing it for so long already and have learned what does and doesn't work.

But the ones that first come into teaching are often people with some idealism. They actually want to make a difference. They are keen to be with kids and are more open to paying attention to them.

I passed a young math teacher's classroom one day. He was only 26 years old. His grade 11 academic math students were all standing up behind their desks row after row of them. Each was massaging the neck muscles of the person in front of them. Then he had them turn around and return the favors the other direction.

I was sold on the guy right away. What a gutsy exercise to do. What's it got to do with math? Why should they have that kind of physical contact in a classroom? What's going on in there Mr. Sanchez? But he was too alive to know any better, to know that teachers don't have their math classes do such things.

And this is the problem. Schools don't really see their students as children or as whole beings. They see the students as cogs in what they are trying to do. As one colleague asserted loudly and proudly, "I teach math!" The curriculum is a Bible. Teachers get paid to teach it. No one stops to ask why or how or what. The curriculum offers safety to all. Principals feel safe if the teacher covers the curriculum. Teachers feel secure knowing each day that they are covering this or that unit from the curriculum. Parents are assured that their kids are learning the curriculum. And the students get grades based on their mastery of the curriculum - poor ones leading to feelings of dejection and good ones leading to elation. All of it is false. Surely, it's an exact replica of how the old Christian world pursued religious inculcation and how the modern, Islamist fundamentalism works. No questions. All a matter of following. The text matters, not the human who it's intended for.

At least with the Bible and the Koran, there's the conviction that they in fact come from God. The curriculum on the other hand is devised by mortals. Mortals who approach it with a tradition base. The past dictates the present. Teachers and professors were all successful at the curriculum they followed as students, thus they reproduce what got them to their station. They ask those who they teach to aim at the same mastery.

Go into any school, sit in an academic classroom and you will feel immediately on familiar ground. Except for the latest technological gadgetry, what the kids are learning about, what they are doing for assignments, how the teacher is teaching all will be just what it was thirty years before. And thirty years before it would have been the same as the thirty years before that. Educators reproduce what they had. The content changes only as new scientific facts are discovered.

In days past, the students were simply told to memorize so they could answer all the questions on tests. That was equated to learning. Now we do different activities that are designed to help the students memorize, so they can answer all the questions on tests.

There is no questioning of this fundamental driving process. If it's good enough for churches and religion, it must be good enough for schools and education. It's all about maintaining comfort zones.

Students are living hours of their lives each day in intellectual dead zones. Strong statement? Yep. Overstated? I hope so. But let's look at how the kids behave and feel in their classrooms. The most telling sign is what happens when a semester ends. 90% of all the students chuck their notebooks in the garbage. The class is over: the marks are finished; phew!. Next class. If there was genuine value in what had taken place in those classes, the students would overwhelmingly keep their notebooks, their assignments, their tests - keep the outward symbols of what they had learned. Instead, it's "I got through it." And the teacher often feels the same.

Where is the vibrancy, the immediacy? I often ask classes this question. "If you could get full credit for a high school education and be able to stop right now, how many would take the credit and quit?" Guess how many say they would? 90%! They are bored in their classes. They understand the uselessness of them. They might parrot the slogans, but they don't believe them. A lawyer friend of mine once said, "There's justice, and then there is the law." I'll say, "There is education, and then there is what happens in schools."

Without a doubt, the main attraction of schools is that the kids get to be with their friends and with other kids. It's social. The notion that learning ought to be the attraction can only be true if learning is what schools are about. It isn't. Kids are not taught to think, to reflect, to ponder, to pursue deep thoughts, to critically analyze, to imagine, to explore, to innovate, to go outside the box, to go beneath the surface. Sometimes a teacher might tell them to do those things, but they won't be taught how, nor will they be given time to engage in anything that leads to those outcomes. Classes are about doing assignment after assignment, always linearly moving forward, adding up marks, posting marks, getting the right answers.

Homework is the symbol of everything that's haywire about our way of doing schools. The kids spend six plus hours in class after class, expected to absorb and comply and, above all, PAY ATTENTION! Then, their reward is to put more time in at home! What fun! And what an indicator that there is no awareness of the human being at those student desks. And homework assignments are usually as boring, repetitive and stultifying as the ones in class. It's all about keeping them busy. All about salving the teacher's and school's need to pronounce that they are setting high expectations. It's all about control and compliance.

For ten years, I ran a peer counselling class. From those grade 10 and 11's who applied to the program, I would select out a group of fifteen to twenty and train them that spring so they could then function as official peer counsellors the following year. My training was a two-hour class once a week after school. It was intense and demanding.

Being a peer counsellor meant the student was declaring themselves to be a person who was trained in rudimentary counselling skills and who would listen to, care about, be real with, and keep confidences with any other student who was struggling with any issue. My program had two major components. I taught them basic counselling skills, some psychology, and some awareness of the panorama of issues that beset us humans - sexual abuse, substance abuse, suicide, loneliness, mental illness, peer pressure, etc. The second component was self-knowledge and personal risking. Each training session would have an exercise in which they would have to think about and open up to themselves. Some examples: I would have them take turns holding each other. I would have them make pictures of a sad event in their background. I would have them talk with each other about their parents.

At the end of each week's training session, everyone would sit on the floor to participate in a sharing circle. The instructions were that each would speak if they chose to. They could talk about whatever they wanted as long as it was real and meant something to them. It could be about something that had hurt them in the past, something that happened that day which bothered them, something joyful that was occurring. It didn't matter as long as they felt it had substance and meaning. Speaking was voluntary, and most important of all, no one was allowed to answer back, they could only listen. And afterwards no one was to bring up what was said with that person or anyone else. The speakers themselves were free to invite further discussion of their issue after the training session was all over. During the sharing circle, it was a free time to be heard unconditionally. The point was that if they expected others to open up to them once they were peer counsellors then they had better be able to open up to someone else. In other words, be able to walk the talk.

Inevitably those sharing sessions were rich, sometimes raw, and always worth it. I would share also. Testament to their value to the students was the behaviour of a student named Bill. During the training year, I would not allow anyone to miss more than one class. Thus, kids would have to really juggle their schedules. A drama teacher was once very angry that her actress was missing an afterschool drama class because she "had to go" to the peer counselling training. The girl was quite willing to drop out of the drama if she had to. In the year that Bill was already a peer counselor, training sessions were not as frequent nor attendance so compulsory. Bill was a rugby player. On the surface, a rugged, macho type of kid. In rugby season, he would often miss most of a session because of his rugby commitments, but he always cut those short and showed up for the sharing circle. Bill would come in all sweaty in his rugby uniform and cleats. Down on the floor he would sit with the rest. Never fail.

The point I am making is that the peer counselling program meant something to the students. They saw it as heavy, as personally beneficial, as making a difference, as stimulating. It treated them as whole beings with pasts and with a multiplicity of components in their lives. It invited them to be themselves. I could have kept it safe. I could have not included the personal part, the risking. Had I done so, it would have become just another class and likely forgotten about in the same way.

I followed a similar practice with the peer counsellor program as I do when I counsel kids individually. I ask for feedback. I have an idea when I start, I have a plan, but I know that the crucial factor is how it's working, how it's being received. Am I hitting the mark? That's the huge hole in schools today. We don't ask the kids, and if we do, we don't listen and take their direction. We find reasons what they say can't work.

It should not be about the school or about the teacher. It should be all about the kids. Is the student learning? What are they learning? What is the relevance, the benefit of that learning? Will it serve the student? What aren't they learning that the changing world would suggest they need to learn? We are afraid to get those answers. No one likes to face their own failure or incompetence. The system does not want to be faced with its bankruptcy. So we don't ask.

The number one essential characteristic of a course and a classroom is that it should be engaging. If the students are involved and intellectually and emotionally engaged then you can be sure meaningful learning is taking place. Those dance students mentioned earlier - they were engaged. There is some silly premise that academics, that intellectual pursuits are a chore. Of course, the kids are bored. Of course, it's dry. There's no other way. They have to learn that stuff. Hogwash. All is an excuse to keep doing what we teachers feel comfortable with.

A grade eleven student from Korea asked me for help with his social studies assignment. It was from a textbook. It was some questions on the pioneer days. I read through the material with him trying to add to and fill out the story. He understood and looked up at me with this open, intelligent expression, "but I don't care about any of that".

He was from Korea. I smiled at him and replied, "I know. None of the other students do either."

He tilted his head, smiled, and politely said, "Then why do we have to learn it?"

I tilted my head, smiled and said, "Because that's the way it is."

What's wrong with this scenario is that he was right. It makes no sense. The students follow the textbooks. The teacher teaches the textbook. Bible studies but no Jesus, no God.

Staff meetings are a favorite of every teacher. No one wants to miss them. I'm joking. They do reveal something, however. Staff meetings are considered vital to the smooth and proper functioning of a school. They are a time when everyone can get together and share ideas or engage in the formulation of the school's direction. Yet, unless there is the rare, particularly hot issue, no teacher has the slightest hesitation to skip out. During the meeting, which can sometimes stretch over an hour, teachers yawn, chat asides to each other, fidget, throw things, doze off, and daydream. Some do marking. Some go up for an extra cookie from the plate set at the entrance to ease the pain of the meeting. Some just patiently wait for it to end. Hmmm?

And no teacher feels critical of themselves or their fellows for this behaviour and approach to their own "vital" learning. The same behaviour from their students would evoke criticism and consequences. Not acceptable. The students are supposed to be there to learn. If the principal talks too long at the staff meeting, he/she is boring and attention spans drift - that's okay, that's normal. If the principal tries any cute exercises, then it's "that's inane" and "why are we doing this?"

But the students? Sit up in your desk. Pay attention. This is important. I'm going to keep you after class!

The teachers know themselves to be whole people who have lives and commitments after school. The students somehow are different.

Classes are boring and hopeless because they are sedentary and one-dimensional. They are not engaging because too often the subject matter is dated, has no relevance to the real lives of these students now or in the future, is delivered in an unstimulating fashion, is accompanied with too many arbitrarily decided requirements, or just simply does not fit the clientele. Our kids are martyrs in this system. Their lives are filled with drudgery day in and day out.

The ones who fail have a false sense of their own capabilities. The ones who flourish have a false sense of the value of their accomplishments. A student I taught grade 9 English to came back to see me about a psychology project she was doing in her third year of university. Part way into our meeting, she looked me in the eyes and asked me if I thought kids were taught to think in high school. I answered that I didn't and she nodded. "I just this year started to think. I didn't realize until this year that I had never yet learned to think." I felt sad.

When I first started teaching, a fifteen-year-old aboriginal boy was a real keen student in my alternate program, which was designed to challenge and develop kids who had failed in the regular classroom. He couldn't read. He felt a great deal of shame about it. All the others in the program could read. So, logically he concluded that it was because something was wrong with him. He must be stupid. Soon after I met him, we had a breakthrough of sorts. I asked him the question, "Ted, did you ever think that the reason you can't read isn't because of you but because the teachers you have had just didn't know how to teach you?" His face contorted into shock. This was the one conclusion that no one had ever posited. From that moment onward, we went forward.

Of course, it is all too true. No one fares worse than those in the system who have significant learning disabilities. Over and over, they get confronted with their failures to succeed, and over and over again they get expectations thrown at them that make no sense. I liken it to yelling at a deaf person and then penalizing him because he couldn't comply. The fallback view is that the kid is lazy. "If he would put his mind to it, he could do it." Sounds good but speaks more of our own inability.

The truth is that too many teachers doing the learning assistance for those kids that need it just don't have the specific expertise to remediate them. They don't know how to teach the kid so that the kid develops the missing skills. I know because I have had learning assistance classrooms in the past and I was useless to those kids. My class was like the great majority of all the learning assistance classes, it was a homework class, a catch-up class, in which the focus was helping the students get their bloody assignments done no matter how off base those assignments were, no matter how useless.

The thinking is that by keeping the student at grade level, it helps them to feel better, and they can stay with their peers. That could be okay if real learning was occurring by going that route. Instead, it's filling notebooks with quickly forgotten work, it's pushing the kid to dig a hole then fill it in again. What the kid needs in order to really catch up doesn't happen. Few know how to set that kind of interaction up. And if they try then the kid can kiss good-bye his grade level.

What I did was try to make the classroom as warm and friendly as possible. And I tried to develop a meaningful relationship with the students. I figured if I was going to enable the kid to float along with the rest then I might as well make it positive. I knew I wasn't really helping in any significant way.

If I had been given free reign to really tackle it as best that I could, with my limited expertise and training, I would have taken a different direction. As it is, schools are filled with hierarchies. I once got in a shouting match in an English department meeting soon after I started at a school. I was balking at following along with what had been decided on as the practice for that department - the scope and sequence - wonderful buzzwords that pretend to guarantee consistency and progression from year to year. I didn't want to teach the grammar sheets and the vocabulary sheets that were assigned by the department for the grade I had. THE WAY IT'S DONE HERE should be posted above the entrance to every school.

My sin was wanting to base vocabulary assignments on the vocabulary that emerged in the stories they were reading, and have the grammar instruction stem from the writing the students did.

So, when a teacher takes on a learning assistance class he knows he had better fit in to what the model for that school is.

Had I the courage to buck the rules or if I was scheduled to be more of a full time learning assistance teacher, I would have brought all the parents of the students in for a meeting. I would have told them that I didn't know enough to genuinely help their kids change and develop the skills they were missing. I'd ask if I could recruit from the community to get in volunteers to help. I do think that the only way to break the hold of the learning disability - and that disability could be emotional as well as intellectual - is to get as much one-to-one engagement as possible. Especially with attention deficit disordered kids, I think an answer is to get them constantly attended to by a caring adult. Then it would be concentrated reading and writing practice with instant feedback. I know that when I sit one on one with a kid, they pay attention and they learn, they advance. But then I need to leave them for another student and the advancing stops.

So, I'd go to the community for volunteers and I'd fill the learning assistance classroom with these helpers. I'd find ways for them to all have lunches together. I'd have food and drink in the classroom. I'd tell the regular teachers that the kids were not going to be following along with the rest of the students they were teaching. I'd have them pursue an alternate curriculum, one based in language skills development, in thinking development, in criticism, in analysis, and in personal involvement. And I would insist that they get credit for the English 8 or the Social Studies 9 or whatever course they were going to be short because of what they were doing in the learning assistance classroom.

"But what about all the stuff they would miss? How can you give them credit when they didn't do the work? It's not fair to those who did. This is a double standard." Nonsense. It's all just stuff. Stuff that has no intrinsic worth. The engagement, the thinking, the growth are what matter. The stuff is all interchangeable. The only subject this doesn't apply to is math. That's another story. And as far as fairness, if it's unfair to those doing the regular "stuff" then maybe it's an indication that the regular "stuff" is something to be avoided, otherwise it would be desirable and then it would be the poor kids in learning assistance who would be missing out on the excitement.

Learning assistance teachers at least know that all kids are different, that they learn differently, that they bring a variety of issues to the classroom every day. Regular classroom teachers have 20-30 students to take care of for four or more classes every day. An English teacher might be teaching 120 students in a semester. There is no way they can see the students as complex kids, each possibly needing a varied approach in order to achieve learning. So they turn away from that reality. They focus on what they want to teach and they shove it to the students. Those that it fits, good for them, and those that it doesn't fit, too bad, that's life.

Take the rush out of the dynamic. Scrap the slavish obedience to the curriculum. Humanize it all. Slow it down, relax, and start talking with the kids. Get to know them. Get them involved in designing and exploring what is to take place each day. They know their world. They don't have an adult's experience or greater vision, so together the teacher and students can create an exciting learning environment that is tailored to the particular needs of everyone in the class. Make it fun.

In the old days, showing a film was a guaranteed way to get everyone absorbed. Then the video machine did the same job. Now, with the proliferation of every manner of technological wonder, audio-visual offerings are running a poor race. Kids have been exposed to so much; their adrenalin levels are so much higher. It is far more difficult to wow them, to draw them in, to keep their attention with a prop when the subject matter is stale or disconnected from them.

The fear of not covering the curriculum curtails the possibility of any creativity or adventure from the teacher. I taught a grade 9 English class in a room that had a window looking across the valley at a nice mountain. It was maybe 3 miles straight away. I was looking out at it one day and I realized that every day for years and years the students and teachers in this school had in various classrooms looked out at that mountain and probably admired it, especially in the spring. But I suspected that no teacher had every said to his students, "Let's walk straight to the mountain and climb it."

So we did. We weren't going to walk along roads or the regular route to get there but straight towards what we could see. It meant getting permission from other teachers for the students to miss their classes. That happens routinely when team members have to go on road trips, when there is an assembly, when there's a fire drill. It also meant that I had to get permission from some landowners to walk through their property.

The day came. We walked out of our classroom. We walked across the playing fields. The P.E. students stared at us, wondering where we were going, why no one had gym strip on if we were outside during school hours. We walked to the end of the school property and down through a field. We crossed a fence. One girl caught her coat on a barb. We trundled through a farmer's property. No one was there except an old dog. He had a grey beard and barked with a hesitant, far-off bark, but his old tail wagged. He knew we were on a quest. Chickens scattered.

Down that farmer's driveway we trod, skipping over the odd puddle. Jim got his foot muddy. So did Kerry. We came out onto the road, crossed it, and went up a bank and through another field. Another fence. Another farm. Then along a long dirt road that eventually circled and took us to a farm at the base of Mount Swanson. Then up. No path. No signs other than the blue above us.

We went up. The whole idea was to point and say, "Let's go there." After ninety more minutes, everyone arrived at the summit, each finding their own route. It was bright, sunny, a slight breeze. We ate our lunches. Then we went all the way down. Several kids tumbled or tripped on deadfall on the way down.

At the bottom, we had to wait for three boys who got lost a bit. And then, before we knew it, we were back at the school. Everything was just as we had left it. No one had missed us. But each of us was different. Each of us felt as though we had done something. Something out of the ordinary. Something with no purpose, with no "learning outcome", with no marks. Something that nobody else had done or even considered. We all knew that we had gone on a journey. We had changed ever so slightly. And we were all tired out.

I think of that little escapade as a metaphor. We so seldom look at what we can do, at what it is easily possible to do. In education, we are well programmed, all of us. And we tend to stay on the track despite the thrill of the mountains all around us.

So, the foundation of our schools could be asking kids what they need, what turns them on, what fits. It could be involving them, charging them with a significant role in planning and delivering what is decided to be the best learning. This means giving away some control. It means joining with the kids rather than doing all the telling. It means using the curriculum as a rough outline. Very rough. It means being creative and having fun and forgetting about time. It means calculating success by meaningfulness.

Several teachers in various schools I've been in have had a rule that anyone coming late to their class had to wait outside the locked door until it was convenient for the teacher to let them in. That might be as much as the entire period. It was to teach the kids punctuality and to value their class. Hmmm, I wonder who locks the door when the teacher is held up because the principal has approached her in the hall for a brief chat?

There is a backward and unacceptable double standard. That's what the need for control does. It leads into a sense of entitlement. A vice principal had to deal with Barry. After school that day, Barry had told the science teacher, Mr. Larson, "Fuck you!" Mr. Larson had brought him down and he wanted consequences. The vice-principal spent twenty minutes with Barry and then sent him home for the next day. Mr. Larson was angry. "One day! How can you call that discipline? You're making a big mistake, and you sure as hell aren't standing up for your teachers!"

The vice-principal was calm. "Mr. Larson, I understand you are upset. And I don't think that Barry's choice of language is acceptable at all. Normally, I would have suspended him for a longer duration, but I felt that my hands were tied just a bit. Barry immediately admitted that he had sworn at you, but as we talked he explained how he was in the back of your classroom looking at the posters you have on the wall. He said that you came in and noticed that one had been torn at the bottom. You came over and accused him of doing it, and when he protested that he had done no such thing, you called him a 'little, scum-sucking liar'. That's when he swore back at you."

Mr. Larson did not see how the vice-principal's hands were tied.

I prefer Mr. Norman's approach to kids. He was a man who started his teaching career later in life, sometime in his mid-thirties. His specialty was wood shop. He also taught design and technology. One year, he was asked to teach two grade eight social studies classes. He had never taught social studies. In fact, I'd have to say his English writing skills were not all that good either. Mr. Norman was a hands-on kind of guy. His shop classes were always interesting and the students enjoyed them.

The rest of the staff gulped when he was assigned two blocks of social studies, especially those of us who knew his writing limitations. Plus, he was older, now in his forties. There were going to be academic expectations, more stress, and a totally different classroom configuration.

But just as they say with teenagers, attitude is everything, and Mr. Norman rose to the occasion, or maybe he just did what came naturally. Instead of taking the textbook and curriculum as authorities, he looked at the major topic areas and adapted. Wisely, he understood his own strengths and his own style, so he did what gave him success in the shop, he made the course hands-on. He got the students moving. In the classroom, and out of it. Just the way they would in the shop.

The unit on ancient civilizations did not focus on note taking. The students were asked to bring their favourite meats or vegetables, and then the class went out to the forested part of the field at the back of the school, lit bonfires and roasted the food with sticks. They ate it with their hands.

The Crusades unit focused on building medieval armor and weapons and engaging in jousts and other duels. Each other unit also became kinetic - centred on doing, on activity that was engaging and fun, but took effort and engineering.

Mr. Norman instinctively understood that teens need movement and the younger the teens, the more need for movement. Forcing them to sit in a chair for an hour and then another hour and then another hour every day for ten months is a guarantee of dullness. Like the adults in the staff meeting, their minds can take only so much before switching off. We all know this about ourselves. Yet we continue the same process year after year in every high school. It's a misguided attempt to override nature. We think we can force-feed kids. Go into any academic classroom, and if the teacher has had the students sitting for over half an hour - often before that even - sitting and listening, then you will see a classroom of eyes that are glazed over. Their minds will be elsewhere and the lesson will be entering through a fog. The keeners will be the few to be on task.

The remedy that many teachers employ is to assign seatwork. The kids read, do questions, or take notes. All are taxing and create lethargy and a drain of enthusiasm. Retention is minimal. Meaningfulness is minimal. The teacher only does this because that's how it was in his classroom when he was a student and because he doesn't know anything else to do. The curriculum says cover such and such topics. THE KIDS HAVE TO GET IT DONE, right? Slug through it.

Writing notes and seatwork does work like a charm though in terms of discipline and classroom management. The kids go quiet, the teacher

can sit back and relax and it looks like "work" is being done. Any colleague, or administrator, or parent peeking in would smile and say good
job. In reality, it's busy work. I experimented once with what the students were actually getting from the notes I wrote on the board. First, I
wrote in a long line right across the chalkboard and then continued the
sentences onto a large cardboard box that was sitting atop a filing cabinet
beside the board. I wrote on each face of the box that they could see and
then went back to the start of the chalkboard to continue the next line of
notes. No one said a word. They got out of their seats so they could read
the sides of the cardboard box and kept on writing. A few snickered but
no one questioned it. The notes were what mattered.

And did they? At other times, I have been writing notes and in the
midst of the paragraph begun to write gibberish, sentences that had
no connection or made no sense with the topic. No one said a word.
They just kept on writing. It was all mechanical. All following along. No
thinking or engagement. Across the country are notebooks and notebooks filled with writing that will likely never be looked at again, will
mean little, and will find their way into garbage cans. But you sure get a
nice quiet classroom.

There is too much to remember anyway. We've never had such a
flood of knowledge and information. No one can master even the tiniest
amount. That's why the focus in classrooms ought not to be on knowledge
as such. It ought to be on meaningfulness. In my own grade eight class
decades ago, I learned - had to memorize - all the monarchs of Britain in
order from the start of the Tudor dynasty in 1497 to the current monarch
in the Hanoverian, now called Windsor, dynasty. What on earth for?

So often, our academic examinations are all about memorization. If
the student can memorize well, we equate that to achievement and learning. Understanding and usefulness are not the issue. But when memorization is what dominates, the teaching is easier. The teacher gets to say,
"Well, we covered all the material in the curriculum. I did my job."

Some facts are necessary. They are the rudimentary building ones
upon which we can then understand and make sense of what happens
around us. We need to know, for instance, that without sufficient iron in
our bodies we can become anemic. We need to know what anemic feels
like. We don't need to know that the chemical symbol for iron is Fe. Nor
do we need to know about its structure, its atomic weight, etc.

Because our concept of curriculum is driven by tradition, security,
and vested interests, it dictates the whole sequence of high school educa-

tion. When students enter grade eight they are in that vortex. It is assumed they all need to know all the information which leads to the final grade twelve outcome. That outcome is a fixed version of "knowledge". But it's all a guess, and there is a bias to it.

Math and science are taught as though those taking it are university bound in those fields. Thus the need for all the facts and topics which, by any objective perspective, are esoteric, in that the average citizen not directly in the field has no need of them. From the beginning, the curriculum is set up to take the student to an outcome they likely will never need. Similarly with English. How many competent, successful, smart adults know what a gerund is, know the difference between a compound and a complex sentence, and know what a subordinate conjunction is? How many know what assonance means. How many know what Robert Frost was getting at when he wrote, "The Wood-Pile"? And why would they or should they?

As with any church or religion, most educators follow much that is unquestioned. It's simply believed. It is. Shakespeare is an example. For generations, schools have been committed to teaching Shakespearean plays. The problem is that Shakespearean plays are written in Shakespearean English, that is, they're very difficult to understand. I know that I can't understand a good percentage of the script in any play. The use of Coles Notes and other annotated texts has become common in order to address some of the language difficulty.

But what's the point of forcing kids every year to read a Shakespearean play? Is it a modern intellectual version of the Castor Oil practice? Because it's good for them. I like Shakespeare. I find that his use of language is clever. I don't know if I'd feel so positive if I made an objective comparison with all the other possibilities of reading material. I do know that the great majority of kids don't like Shakespeare. Reading the plays is drudgery and achieves almost nothing. They don't engage, they don't care, and they find no special entertainment or learning in them. But they trust us that it must be important, must be "good for them".

The double whammy is in how the students are evaluated when doing a unit on Shakespeare. Memorization. Regurgitating meaningless script. Remembering who spoke what to whom and when. Explaining what it meant. This is a travesty of learning and education.

Teaching the Bhagavad Gita, the works of Shaw, Kahlil Gibran, etc. etc. can all be deemed as "important" as "good for them". These are times when students need only some quick exposure to giants like Shakespeare in order to pique their interest and awareness. Then drop it. They'll go back for greater study if it appeals

If adults need esoteric knowledge, they can look it up. They can make a hobby of it. By golly, that's exactly what they often do. As students progress in school, what they need in academics changes. Smart teaching would pay attention to the learners and try to develop the capacity to learn. Our teaching focuses on trying to fill the students up.

None of this is new. We've understood it all for decades. But we do not act on it. The vested interests in the current structure are too great. We'll stick with safety. We'll bore our kids to death.

Like all young animals, kids need to move about. They have energy to spare. We try to control them and keep them in desks along rows in classrooms and inside the walls. No wonder they play hooky, smoke dope between classes, become addicted to text messaging, and develop depression!

No matter how many workshops teachers go to that reveal the latest research on brain development in adolescents, that talk about emotional intelligence, or student centred learning, those teachers time and time again flip right back to what they came from. Innovations may be tried for a short period, small variations may implant themselves more permanently, but the base way of running the classroom and what is being taught will stay the same.

Too many teachers tend to be fearful people. They fear the kids, they fear the parents, they fear their colleagues, and they fear the administration. This does not inspire risk taking or innovation. If they stick with the decades old practices, they don't have to worry about judgment or failure. They fail to give the kids anything meaningful, but they don't fail in the eyes of other adults. If they weren't so fearful, they would zero in on the emptiness in what they teach, the lack of connection to the needs of the kids, and they would do something different.

This is the other problem. They don't know what different to do. They only know where they came from. When communism fell, all over Eastern Europe there became a conundrum. Who would run things - the factories, the enterprises, the schools, and all the other institutions? Those who struggled all their lives to see the day that the stagnant and repressive regimes fell now had a terrible choice to make. Throw out all the managers, the leaders, and face the reality that everything would stop, or keep the old bosses on? The old bosses were, largely, those who had bought in to the craziness of their system and its lies or who had curried favor with the Party. Either way, they were crucially flawed. The choice was to keep the old bosses.

Thus, universities and schools continued their old communistic ways - curriculum, methodology, relations mostly unchanged. The dissident movements felt they had no other choice. So too our teachers. Sometimes they come out of university with new and fresh ideas, they get jobs in the schools, they look around, aren't so sure about those new ideas because no one else is doing that, and they fall into line relying on what is being done by everyone else and what has always been done.

So, the system is rotten. Kids have little chance of truly learning, of developing deeper, analytical intellects, or of becoming fuller human beings. They are controlled, bored, and kept in the dark about themselves and their world. Poll any group of sixteen year olds and ask them about trans fats, about Martin Luther King Jr., about the Iraq or Afghanistan wars, about who their elected representative is, about the reason for learning any of the mathematics they are studying, about why a cell phone works, or about how to grow a garden. At a minimum, three quarters will give you a blank look.

And God help your kid if they specifically have a different learning style or a disability. Out of luck!

Now, the other side of the coin is that it has never been more difficult to teach kids, to get them engaged in meaningfulness. Even the smartest teachers who have skills and a powerful intent in engaging and developing the minds of their students have their work cut out for them. We have so over-indulged our kids with gadgets and special effects that it is very difficult to compete for their attention. It is very difficult to help them discern what is important and what they truly need from all the other information. They have been flooded non-stop with information since the time they were born. And everything has been made to seem as important as everything else.

Dr. Phil, Oprah, Judge Judy, Mixed Martial Arts carnage, Olympic role models, rappers, and the screen before them every time they switch on their TV or computer are all giving the same message - "This is important. Listen to this." The consequence is practised glazing. The messages all come in and they all go out again. Some stick not because of relevance, but simply by chance or circumstances, or by parental buy-in. Mom likes Dr. Phil so the child does also.

Everyone has something to sell. When a teacher tries to sell their version of importance it's just another sales job. For those kids that come from messed up families and homes it's magnified tenfold. Their heads are half elsewhere all the time. Half of them is locked into the family drama or the family pain. They aren't able to give undivided attention.

PAUL - The P.E. teacher had kicked Paul out of his grade eleven P.E. class. Mr. Green was a tough guy. He saw things the traditional way. He set expectations, demanded that they be met and rewarded them accordingly. He couldn't stand students who he knew weren't trustworthy and who wouldn't give it their best shot. And he seldom wondered or asked why. When there were logical explanations, he'd not much care, simply react that they shouldn't be in P.E.

A twisted ankle might need treatment but you were supposed to suck it up. Paul was a guy who had told Mr. Green that he was going back to the changing room and Mr. Green had discovered him somewhere else. This happened twice. He also sometimes wouldn't play a game with much enthusiasm. Mr. Green told him to find another course.

What he didn't know was that Paul had no father. When Paul was five years old and living in another part of the country, he lost his dad in a particularly unique way. His parents had split up and Paul lived in an apartment with his father. One evening his father was having a big party. There were lots of people, lots of alcohol and drugs. Loud music. Paul loved his dad. His mom lived elsewhere and was remarried.

Paul's dad put him to bed in his room at about 8 o'clock even though the party was in full swing. He fell asleep, but a few hours later arguments broke out. Paul was awakened. He stayed in his room and listened to the yelling. A door slammed. The music continued and everything seemed back to normal. A bit later, he heard the shooting.

The guy who had left in anger lived down the hall. He came back with his gun. He shot to death the several people still at the party, including Paul's father. Paul stayed in his bed, terrified. He pulled the covers over his head and pretended to be asleep. He heard the killer open his bedroom door and come in. He could sense him standing over his bed. Then the man spoke in a voice that Paul could still easily hear all these years later, "I know you're not asleep. But you don't have to worry. I'm not going to hurt you." And then the man left the apartment. After a while, Paul got up and walked out among the dead bodies to find his father.

So, yeah I guess Paul had some problems all right. I guess maybe he was not a settled person inside. After the killing of his father, Paul had gotten some counselling and gone to live with his mother. He didn't get along with her husband, and so later on went to live with his aunt and uncle in our town. He had such bright blue eyes. As a student, he had difficulty fully getting into his assignments. They'd usually be done but with only as much effort as attaining a C required. He still had uneven sleeps. P.E. was important to him because he saw it as a needed stress release and he liked playing the sports. Getting kicked out was a definite problem for him. He felt sorry that he'd blown it with Mr. Green.

Part of the agreement I had with him was that I wasn't to tell the other teachers about what had happened. The privacy was important to him. He also did not want any therapy from me. Ours was a relationship solely to provide a bit of a breather, have a relaxed talk, be a place he could come to. I went to another P.E. teacher and got him to accept Paul into his class.

It's funny because teachers are the first to want to be cut some slack for themselves and each other when trauma hits their families, don't hesitate to stay home when illness strikes, put off marking if they feel extra fatigued on any given day, but when it comes to students so many of them won't extend the same allowances in mitigating circumstances. Or they do so in a partial way. They ease off for a few days or a couple of weeks but then it's presumed the kid should get on with it and behave as though nothing had happened.

I know the teachers are not mean people, but it seems so hard sometimes for them to actively and consistently practice kindness and understanding. I think the religious adherence to the curriculum and to "standards" cause much of the problem. Such a silly obstacle to being human. Most teachers' final grades are calculated by adding up scores on assignments and tests. In the duration of a semester, there might be forty such scores. Missing marks means a lowering of the grade. Common sense would say that a student's level of skill development, of readiness for the next grade, could be concluded by looking at ten or twelve scores.

In English for example, a well-written essay just once shows that a student can write a well written-essay. Math is different because so much of it is sequential, so in fairness to teachers, putting a student through to the next level in math can't really be done unless the student has understood the units. They could be given more time to get it learned, but as long as we make students take math into the higher grades, it will be the one subject that has to be mastered at each level.

Aside from the personal problems, the different learning styles and the disabilities, and even the sidetracking caused by all the technological gadgets, educators face still another significant challenge. We now have a generation of kids that don't care. Our societal level of affluence, our social safety nets, our current fashion of catering to and providing instant gratification to our kids combines to create a false assumption of security. Too many of our kids are no longer strongly motivated to better themselves through learning. The idea of working hard is not a common ethos. The values that awareness, learning, self-development and growth all matter are not commonly held by kids. They don't really feel the need to strive for a full education. Instead, it's something that should be given to them and that they begrudgingly tolerate. They hear the adage, "you can't get anywhere, can't get a good job, without a good education," and they nod their heads but they don't necessarily actively buy into it.

For those whose families are not overly impoverished or dysfunctional, all of their lives they've had things and activities given to them. They've been signed up for soccer, for hockey, for Brownies and 4-H. They've had birthday parties, gone on vacations to far off places. Lots of presents, "memories created" for them by their parents. As styles change, they get the new ones. Lunches are thrown away if the kid doesn't feel like eating. The old is dumped as soon as it gets old. Fifty per cent or more of any classroom has a cell phone and the bills that go with them are paid for.

A common occurrence in many schools is the celebration known as dry grad or super grad. In years past, graduating day meant parties before and after. Sometimes that meant accidents. To interfere with that, schools and parents came up with the plan to hold gala nights in which entertainment and fun could be had until dawn under adult supervision and without booze.

That original motivation is understandable. Unfortunately, many grad groups just focused on providing a memorable and fun splash for their kids. Do it for them. Take care of them.

In developing countries, where kids are lucky to get to go to school, there is a totally different attitude. Compared to our schools there is focus, motivation, and dedication.

The lack of incentive and motivation, the disinterest in intellectual development is a malaise that more and more permeates our youth. The future doesn't exist. It's all now. Security and comfort are taken for granted. All is self-gratification.

As well there is a distinct lack of values. A major reason why some parents opt for private or religious schools is to get their kids in regular contact with values. I'm not sure that's really what happens in those schools on a penetrating level, but they make a better show of it than public schools. Our public schools stick with safe. The notion of values gets equated with teaching religion. We fear that. Mustn't upset anyone. The result is that there is a moral vacuum in schools. Posters get put up. That's it. Elementary schools do a far better job with values. They engage their pupils with environmental and societal issues, with doing for others. At the high school level it's all forgotten about and replaced by an emphasis on courses, grades, and outcomes. No real time for anything else. It's up to extra-curricular clubs that might have an emphasis on values, but their activities are clearly on the fringe, an addendum to what really matters.

None of this is to suggest that private schools, which usually trumpet an emphasis on values and achievement, are better than public schools. Anyone can claim they "teach" values, but is there a truly concentrated practice followed, in which students are stimulated to develop *their own set of values*? Private schools, as often as not, have a particular viewpoint on what values are desirable and what constitutes success. How many of them are committed to developing free and critical thinking, independent activism, or sexual awareness? How many cultivate humility or respect and acceptance for the choices or stations of others? Public schools hold the promise for the future. **But teacher colleges must undergo a dramatic shift in order to train educators who will genuinely respond to the current lived reality of kids and to the wholeness of those developing beings.**

Chris Korytko – 15 years old

In schools, the kids are in the community of all their peers. They face peer pressure, they model, they want to belong, they are powerfully influenced by each other each second for months and months every year until they graduate. To think that there is no place or no need to teach values in such a setting is unbelievably ignorant of how we develop as human beings.

I remember seeing a huge banner taped all along one wall in a school. On it were painted the words, "HANDS AGAINST RACISM". It was set up by the leadership class. The idea was for students to dip their hands in paint and print them on the banner. Once dried, they wrote their names on their handprints. Because I had made a point of teaching workshops on racism to some classes in the school and because I was so familiar with the social workings in the school, I spotted the duality at play. I recognized name after name of kids who I knew to be as prejudiced as any average kid who had not fully been taught differently.

They had put their handprints up because their friends were doing it and because it was fun getting their hands in paint, and because it was fun to see their names on the wall. They also all knew that racism was. Bad. But none really thought about what the whole exercise meant nor thought about their own attitudes and behaviours. The disconnect is so easy and common.

Isn't it a bit bewildering that there is no planned or concerted effort to teach kids: how to resolve conflicts with others, how to cooperate with others, how to communicate articulately and respectfully, to understand and be sensitive to cross-cultural differences, about racism, about sexism, about discrimination against gays, about responsibility, about respect, about the interconnectedness and interdependence of all of us, about morality, about beliefs, about spirituality, about stillness, about the golden rule or honesty or loyalty or fairness or caring or perseverance or commitment or flexibility or adaptability or balance or self-care? The list can go on. We just assume that all that happens naturally. In today's world of busyness, of distraction, of media influence 24/7, of two parents working or one parent depressed and hanging on, the kids are going to get all those values on their own? Magic.

Now, this is a good time to qualify again what and how I've been describing everything. I've overstated it all. Everywhere there are exceptions. Learning does happen. I've overstated it to make a point. Our schools are far too much like this. We go about operating our schools and we interact with our teens with chosen blinders on. I'd like to rip them off.

Isn't there a contradiction when I say that kids are bored because what happens in the classrooms is outdated, out of touch, and poorly taught, and then turn around and say that the kids are bored because they've had too much special effects in their lives, are *gadgetized* and can't be reached, and then that the kids are living in a time when they don't care anyway because they've been given everything? No, what I'm saying is that it's all happening together. The kids are living in a flawed educational world, in the time of their teens, when it's all happening together.

Kind Words...From a Teacher

Excuse me, John, I have a
problem with your essay.
Your R's are backwards,
you spelled ten words wrong,
your writing is too big,
you are writing all in capitals
and your handwriting is messy.
Your letters are squished together
and this essay is incomplete.
Other then that,
It's quite good.

Megan Malashewsky
age 13

Things That have Gone Wrong in 8th Grade

- *Lost best friends*
- *Received threats*
- *Teased (called names)*
  a. People make songs up about me.
  b. Telling false things about me.
  c. Teased about being overweight.
- *Parents fight more often than used to. On a regular basis.*
- *Lost confidence.*
- *I'm now insecure.*
- *Tryed to kill myself 3 times.*
- *Frightened, angry, depressed.*
- *Flunking English*
- *Stuck in P.E. with 4 worst enemies.*
- *Can't trust anyone really.*
- *Ran away when parents were near fighting, stayed with sister and her husband.*
- *I'm too scared all the time.*
- *Can't defend myself.*
- *Cry myself to sleep sometimes.*
- *Grandfather had a heart attack.*
- *Grandmother has stroke.*
- *Mother and father spaz at me every time I do something wrong.*
- *Now best friend's mom hates me.*
- *Parents always tell me how bad I am and that my sister was never as bad as I am.*

Janice – 13 years old

6. The Age Of Empty Vs The Self Within

A few years ago, I wrote a newspaper article about two young Czechs named Mirek and Katka that I had met in Prague. They were vibrantly alive intellectually. They were very knowledgeable about their own history and culture, and they were actively curious about the rest of the world. My article contrasted them with Canadian young people, though they both assured me that they were not exactly typical of the usual Czech youth.

One day while walking with Mirek, who was twenty, he asked me in the middle of our conversation, "Could you live without art?" He was dead serious. That was when I knew for certain that I had to write that article. I cannot imagine a twenty-year-old North American asking me the same question.

Flash forward now to current time. Both have finished their master's degrees, Katka in English and Mirek in theatre production. Katka has married and just had her first baby. She has made two extended camping and hiking trips to Iceland, she teaches yoga classes and has produced a series of DVDs of instructional English. Mirek has started a cultural NGO in his hometown that focuses on promoting cultural activities and doing developmental work with the disadvantaged Roma (gypsy) population in his region. He has worked as executive assistant to the Czech federal minister of minorities. The latter position took him to Ethiopia, Venice, New York City, and Yemen. He is going to seek a position on city council in the next election in order to combat the growing corruption and anti-Roma direction in the current administration.

Both of them could not be more alive, more engaged in the full process of living. I was having a serious discussion with Mirek about schools and education and I asked him what he considered the three most important factors a human needed in order to be truly happy and successful. He answered right away: depth, the capacity to exchange the depth with others, and confidence. We went on to come up with additional factors: sense of self, the ability to understand how we have been created and influenced by our early life experiences and relationships, how to communicate in relationships, how to learn, exposure to a broad array of experiences, resilience, problem solving skills, full access to one's emotions, the capacity for love and empathy, the readiness to embrace challenges, curiosity, and an understanding of how to self-nurture.

Of course, this list could go on, but even a quick reflection should bring nods of agreement that, yep these are meaningful, substantive, and absolutely pragmatic factors that will lead to a happy and successful life. None of them are taught in schools, not focused on, likely not even acknowledged other than by platitude or lip service. Many schools create a mission statement and a list of school goals. Often the composition of these is admirable. But there is no serious application. The day-to-day practice in the school bears no relationship to those goals. As mentioned before, the real priorities are order, compliance, assignment completion, being busy, quiet, and achieving good grades. An "A" is the coveted prize, the accomplishment. What the "A" means, what it is for, how it came to be, what the teacher actually taught, what the measurement standard was, whether or not there was any point to it even - none of this is considered. It doesn't matter. It isn't asked about. The letter on the piece of paper is what matters. That letter is what all look to in order to determine success and happiness.

No wonder we produce generations who struggle, are unhappy, unfulfilled, and disinterested in actively running their own countries.

Kids spend - actually they are virtually forced into it - close to a third of their lives in school classrooms yet they feel little attraction and see little value in what takes place in all those hours. Inevitably, kids will tell you that the best thing about school is being around their friends. The social life and sports are the biggest pluses in most schools.

I remember one teen who was notorious for coming to school each September and then quitting to go to work at the end of each basketball season. The other teachers were incensed at this, "making a mockery of the school". I thought it was great. Basketball is fun. It develops teamwork, commitment, positive attitude, and the capacity for camaraderie. All are pro-social and important life attributes. They are what education needs to strive to produce. As well, while David was in school there was hope for more of the same, that he would develop a broader relationship with education that went beyond his chosen sport. Had the school an iota of alertness and care it would have welcomed him personally with open arms and then worked out an educational program that was geared to keep him beyond basketball season.

As much as anything else, our kids need schools to matter to them. They can only matter if they are in tune with the real needs of the kids. This will obviously change each few years as society changes. Thus, schools and learning needs to be in flux. Teachers need to be in flux. Responding to and anticipating the changing needs.

Teachers are notorious for idealizing and idolizing their filing cabinets, and now computer files. They identify with the material they have collected over their career. Mistakenly they equate themselves, the job they do, and their worth with the body of stuff they have collected - their lesson plans, assignments, photocopies, games, and tests. The problem is that it quickly becomes dated. Kids change, needs change, but the material that is trotted out remains the same, sometimes for decades.

Learning starts with relationships. Kids need and value that more than any paper the teacher can materialize, more than any expertise they have. Similarly, they value innovation and newness. When a teacher relies on the same old-same old because it makes the teacher feel safe, means less work, and produces familiar results, that teacher cheats both herself and her students out of the now. Out of the vibrant connection that can come from living in the now.

Weeks and months and years go by in high schools with no one interacting over issues that take place in the real world other than by giving momentary remarks. A flu pandemic, a disaster in another country, a fire in the community, a war, a raise in taxes, you name it and the coverage that occurs in any sustained way in a classroom is minimal. The opportunity for a teacher to connect with students and analyze, understand ramifications and interdependences, share feelings, delve into underpinnings, extend and reflect upon issues that are right then happening is missed. No time, gotta keep on schedule to "get through" the curriculum. Keep reaching into the file cabinet or folder on the computer to do what we did last year and the year before.

Mr. Sandhu had the practice of standing at his classroom door at the start of each and every class to greet the students as they entered. He always greeted them with a smile and a hello. On occasion he'd reach to tickle one or pat somebody on the back. My guess is that thirty years from now not one of Mr. Sandhu's students will remember a single thing he taught them, but they'll remember being greeted. When kids believe the teacher knows them and cares about them, they try harder. They feel more at ease. They look forward to coming to the class.

Whenever I'm asked what advice I have for new teachers, I distill it to one point. Instead of going into all the theory and expanding on substance, meaningfulness, involvement, diverse approaches, knowing their students, individualizing, and even going outside the box - all of which I believe in - I stick to a basic suggestion that precludes glazing over or forgetting or argument. I say to the new teacher - have fun. It doesn't have to be and ought not to be so serious. Have fun with the students, have fun with what you are teaching and how you do it. If you are having fun you will be relaxed and attentive. You will not be drained and will not become bored or resentful. If you are having fun then students will look forward to being in your class and being around you. After twenty years of teaching, you will go home one day and still look forward to being back the next day because–ta da–you are having fun. To keep having fun, a teacher has to be thinking of newness. Fun means staying fresh and creative.

I got my wife to bring our dog into my English class. I can still hear his toenails tick tick ticking across the classroom floor. She brought him in to do dog tricks for ten minutes. And I got my dog to bark in the classroom. It wasn't on the curriculum.

Students need to be around adult role models who are modeling naturalness and the capacity to build relationships. Computer focused learning can seem efficient but it exerts a terrible cost. Sitting in front of a computer neuters learning and it replaces human relationship. It replaces modeling of character. It engenders accomplishment of tasks at the expense of interacting with complexity. Schools that allow computers to take over are making a serious mistake.

Education that leads to social growth and evolution has to be complex, it has to be human based. When teachers are talking, looking into eyes, immediately reacting with vocabulary, tone, body language to each response or behaviour from a student then full learning is taking place. With relationships and human exchange, full development occurs. Respect, compassion, sensitivity, awareness of others' needs, intuition, and the full range of communication options are developed.

For generations now there have been admonishments about too much television watching. Limit the amount your kid spends watching TV. Assess the programs and determine which are adult. Studies were presented showing how many violent acts a child witnessed on TV in a year. The effects of all the advertising were articulated. Doesn't this all seem rather quaint now? Almost like the good old days. What a simpler time. What a simpler, easier mentality. Tsk tsk, too much television.

We are in the age of the new worldwide religion. It is called consumptionism. Instead of praying, we buy stuff. And the leading stream in this worldwide religion is worship of the gadget. Of technological devices. Our children are immersed in the private and electronic world of immediate everything.

As soon as something is advertised, kids want it and try to get it. Styles and the latest models provide the buzz in lives. As a consequence, kids become fiddlers. Not the wholesome violin variety but the keyboard kind. Games, texting, Twittering, and updating one's Facebook pages occupy an enormous amount of time and mental musings. Listen to sports heroes and they talk about their love for video games. Even the Pope is on Twitter. The message to kids growing up is full speed ahead. All is cool and wonderful.

I was in a children's playground recently. There were kids everywhere, all having a great time - with the climbing, the spinning, and the swinging and with each other. Mostly it was the moms who were attending their offspring. But there were also four dads and what looked like a grandfather. Be darned if at one time all five of the men were talking on their cell phones!

The great American poet, Lawrence Ferlinghetti was recalling a catchphrase of the late 1960's that was coined by Baba Ram Dass - "Be Here Now", and he observed that the modern catch-phrase seems to be "Be Somewhere Else". We have abetted our kids in this frantic need to be so constantly absorbed within gadgets. Personal technology has taken over.

We have been successfully marketed. Computers are a staple in every school - always being replaced as their designed obsolescence occurs. Cell phones are a staple in every home, always being replaced as their designed obsolescence occurs. Video play stations are sought by every child and then replaced as designed obsolescence occurs. The same with the music gadgets. What message does this imprint on our children? Always chasing the latest. Having to have it. Cost be damned. No one questioning the effects either short term or long term. What does this disinterest in questioning model to our teens?

We have created an era of complacency and acceptance. For all intents and purposes a monolithic lifestyle based on acquiring and speed and continuous gratification focused on objects and superficiality. Even travelling to far off lands has been co-opted into the consumptive understanding. Our young people set off to "do" Thailand, to get through as much of Europe as their Eurail Pass will allow in the weeks they have allotted. Nothing happens in schools to offer a different slant. Nothing is offered to assist a teenager to make sense of this new lifestyle. No debate occurs. No questioning. How sad is that? How contradictory to the core purpose of education? No debate.

There are immense negatives that arise from this new gadget age. As mentioned before, computers mechanize and flatten instruction in schools. They narrow the interactive interface. Instead of being involved in a full examination or presentation of any issue in which a teacher and peers weigh in to understand it from various angles, all the time there being the opportunity to ask for clarification, for additional information, and to posit doubts, the computer feeds out the issues in a static, one dimensional fashion.

While it is faster to go to a computer for information when composing reports or essays, and there is a greater volume of information, the student interaction with the information is often flawed. The quickness and the flatness of the screen evokes a more superficial understanding. The teen as often as not scribbles down facts and ideas as fast as they can in order to complete the assignment. The source is not doubted. If it's on the screen then it must be true. Thus, I've had students research the death penalty on the computer and come up with the most outrageous reports. Biased material sits right alongside objective data in their handed-in work, much of it copied verbatim.

On the other hand, the slowness required to sit with hard copy reading materials lends itself to mental digestion. There is more processing and more retained meaning to what is researched. Computers can be used to expedite getting explicit factual information. But involved interaction is rare with teenagers unless.... unless it is centred on games, special effects, social networking, music or videos.

Their young minds are oriented to play. Today, gadgets mean play. Not generally the kind of play that feeds their development. But a play that steals time, steals relationships, and steals stillness. There is more and more disturbing research that indicates that I.Q. levels are dropping, that attention spans are becoming shorter, vocabularies are shrinking, and sustained reading is falling off dramatically.

All of this is logical. Why read if the images come to you? Why read when constant oral and visual titillation can so graphically come from pressing buttons? But what happens to the parts of our brain that are exercised and nurtured by the imaginative interaction with ideas and plots and characters that appear in print? That's where our capacity for complex, reflective, evaluative, imaginative mental acuity is formed. It is similar to the notion of not using one's left arm and hand for years. It atrophies.

And what of emotional development? We grow emotionally by interacting with others in a wide variety of circumstances, by modeling from peers and elders, by engaging in substantive, meaningful, and challenging discussions and behaviours. To shift the natural tendencies of kids from a multi-textured involvement with others to the flatness of their cell phones and the computer monitor is a recipe for truncation of their essential fullness. Their being.

If a teen constantly communicates by texting short, choppy messages rife with abbreviations, emoticoms, always based on immediacy and the moment, then how can they develop sophisticated vocabulary or thinking? How can they develop insight, analysis, reflection, or complex, deep thinking? Why would they want to? And we've given it all our blessing. Both the practice and the outcomes. Go for it.

There is always the claimer that there hasn't been enough evidence of these "harmful" effects. That there are some positive outcomes. Sure, finger and reaction skills and speeds would have to improve mightily if a person spends hours each day working on them. Similarly, figuring out how to complete the tasks on the screen. No question. But it shouldn't take a rocket scientist nor umpteen studies or a passage of decades to compile data to conclude what common sense tells us directly. If you don't use it then you lose it. If you go away from emotions, complexity, depth, and human texture then you lose it.

It's as asinine as the old debate about violence on TV or in games and movies. "Where's the proof that it's harmful?" has been the shout. Of course those who stand most to gain by refusing to look at harmful consequences in all these case are the ones who stand to profit from the sales of the merchandise and the sales of the lifestyles. Also the parents who, for whatever reason, need to have their kids so engaged. It defies intelligence to believe that a child or teen who grows up being constantly exposed to graphic violent scenarios will not at the very least be more desensitized to it than someone who has not had that exposure. The same child will have been normalized to violent interactions and be more comfortable with a violent reality. That makes a violent reality more acceptable and infers that there will be less motivation by those people to work against a violent society or neighborhood becoming a norm. And logically, it follows that any child who has endured unfair suffering will have modeled through the media exposure a solution for how to deal with conflict. The rage that so often simmers in those who have been victimized will have been shown a method for articulation. Just as morality tales are used to teach sound values, so the slasher movies, the aggressive, violent interactive video games teach the power of that kind of behaviour.

And we haven't even come close to definitively evaluating if there might be harmful physiological effects from the use of cell phones and other electronics because they haven't been around long enough.

But let's just stop a bit and think about the insistence that the internet and the cell phone has brought us all closer together. That the leap in communication capacity has been a boon for human interaction. It is true that for the first time individuals from nations across the globe can have daily and easy contact with each other. It is true that all of us now have the opportunity to know more about each other's nations and experiences. In our history this has never before been the case. Pen pals were once so desperately valued because of the connections they provided within an isolated world.

On a political level this new connectedness surely does mean positive outcomes. Global linking can mean that a repressive state can no longer act without at least some discretion. It means aid can be made available more directly. The connectedness must give hope to so many locked in undesirable conditions or stuck inside repressive regimes. And it means students can also be players in the world. It puts us all closer together.

Yet despite all these positives and potentials, most teenagers in North America are basically as ignorant about their world outside their own neighbourhood as ever before. Maybe more so. The constant connectedness is extended to their own circle and their own limited interests. Thus it merely gives them a more enmeshed and more confined world solely catering to them. Ironically for teens, "other" has perhaps never been more distant.

The choppy text messages that are exchanged do little to give texture to personal connections. They give an illusion of connectedness. Their frequency masks their superficiality and limitedness. Texting precludes complex relationships and maybe more important, it precludes understanding the complexity of self, of others, and of the nature of relationships.

Facebook and other social web sites become viral in popularity and no more specifically than among teenagers. Similar to the need to fit in as far as the latest clothing styles, so too the need to fit in with the latest virtual styles. The uncontrolled public exposure from having a Facebook site brings risks for exploitation and predation that have been often remarked on and written about, but what isn't discussed with any fanfare is the very idea of kids making their lives so public. In some respects we've set it up and encouraged teens to enter into a form of public nudity. On occasion, literally.

Any examination of Facebook pages quickly shows that they are geared to the superficial. Identities are being cast in superficial terms. Teens spend all that time interfacing with and constructing superficial reflections of themselves. Where is the heart in that? Where is the meaning in that?

Again it comes back to schools in the sense that schools can be the counter to the driven and exploited reality that our adult world pulls kids into. Schools **can** be all about meaning, about extracting meaning from events, issues, and surroundings. By their construct, computers and gadgets are not about meaning. They are not about substance. I watch generations of teenagers growing up without having to wrestle with meaning. What has true meaning for them? What has true meaning in life? How do we determine, discern, relate to, and place meaningfulness in our time on the planet?

Meaning equates to depth. The inundation of information on the internet, the access to everything leaves kids unable to know what matters and what doesn't. They are not taught the skills or mindset needed to make sense of the inundation, to go beyond the surface, to see and hear with insight. These are generations that are moving into adult years without a clear sense of what a meaningful life is, what a purposeful life is. Seeking pleasure and parroting out platitudes they've encountered comprise the core of their existence.

In past generations, economic and technological constraints combined to usher generations of the young into survival, work, and family paradigms. To grow up to raise a family, earn a decent living while working honestly, and to join in with a community was the central, unifying ethos that was internalized. It worked. There were convenient limits and convenient ignorances that supported those paradigms. Now the genie is out of the lamp and everything is possible, everything goes.

Such bedrock principles as the value of honesty, of respectfulness, of interdependence, of fairness, of activism are faint in the world of our teenagers. Faint, meaning they may be mentioned but there is no sub-stantive processing of what they entail. In short, our teens are growing up without these values being either taught or reinforced in any active, sustained, or thorough way. We leave it to chance that these values will be significant in any observable form. The talk will be there but no walk-ing the talk.

When so much time and energy is given over to gadget interaction, then it follows that time and energy cannot go to depth, to values build-ing, to complexity in relationships, self-awareness, or thinking. If this all sounds very bleak, it's because it is.

I attended a workshop about the internet's dangers and its perva-sive negative influences on kids. By the end of the presentation I was in shock. A colleague and I, whose intelligence I greatly respect despite us being on opposite sides of the political spectrum, looked at each other and shook our heads. We agreed that it's hopeless, that we've gone too far without knowing the outcome, without the checks and balances needed. Our kids were doomed, we concluded. We could see that there was no way that an ever growing number of kids would not become shaped and driven by the unfiltered exposure to graphic, insidiously manipulative, and negative materials and opportunities at their fingertips. He even lik-ened the gadget addiction to narcotics addiction, saying he thought the needle was already in too deep. Each person willingly contributing a tithe to the cell phone providers in perpetuity.

Intuition and experience tells me that was too bleak. We may be doomed, but we as humans are seldom able to see the full picture, and the mechanics of life are always changing which allows for newer and un-expected developments. In other words, there is hope. We might come to our senses and figure it out.

Victor Frankl, the psychotherapist who survived the Nazi death camps in World War 2, wrote a seminal book called MAN'S SEARCH FOR MEAN-ING. In it he related how the critical component that helped people survive the brutality and hopelessness of the concentration camps was the capacity to retain a sense of purpose. Those who had the conviction that their lives had meaning, that their survival was needed because there was a purpose for them had an edge in resilience and endurance. Their inner sense of meaning gave them strength to continue. Frankl deduced from these experiences that those with emotional or psychiatric difficulties needed to cultivate a sense of meaningfulness in their lives. That the lack of meaning was underlying their varying illnesses, depressions, and unhappiness.

Ferlinghetti stated that our aim seems now to be somewhere else rather than being present in the immediate reality. He wasn't even referring to the virtual reality video games that are so popular. Such games are powerfully attractive to many. They allow the players to create new identities of which they have total control. Similarly to chat rooms and MSN Messenger the individual at the controls can be in actual control of their virtual and cyber lives.

For the many who have lived with too much powerlessness this might give them at least some glimpse of their power to be as they'd like to be. It might foster some confidence or a vision of possibilities. It also, in the case of chat lines, allows for relationships of a kind in which flaws and hang-ups, in which the internal emotional bruises are held at bay. This is positive. So too for lonely kids. They get to have relationships. Others know they exist. They feel they have something. I know one boy, a seventeen year old, who literally has no flesh friends. He spends his time totally alone except for his mom, baby sister, and grandmother, plus the occasional visitors they get. He telephones no one and speaks to no one else. When he comes to school, his interaction with teachers and peers is as minimal as he can make it. He attends sporadically. But he does have two friends on-line in another town who he has never seen. Clearly they are important. They are a link to future possibilities. They mean hope. They mean something.

The problem is that the cyber friendships and the virtual identities are not emanations of the lived identity of the teenager. They are the phenomena of a double or split life. While they can influence social growth depending on the specifics of their exchange, they are just as likely to allow for suppression of and a non-resolution to the lived realities. They don't likely lead to wholeness or growth from the inner core. Instead they are an overlapping or a splitting.

But these cyber connections and graphic video identities are powerfully alluring, as addictive as any other drug in so many ways. They provide absorbing and instant immersion in a reality outside and different from oneself. They are the ultimate of "Being THERE now." That's why I see them as costing far more than they reward. For all the entertainment value, for all the cure for loneliness or victimization experience that they provide, they also steal time and energy from true possibility. They are a vote of non-confidence in the lived identity. A form, almost, of resignation, of giving up. The focus becomes aimed at the better world. The false world.

This is a subtraction from the needed exchanges that await us all in the true world. It is those exchanges that build us. For as we encounter all manner of negative experience, all manner of pain and dejection, we also encounter the positives, the contributing, uplifting occurrences. More than anything else with teenagers this is a theme that needs exposure and reinforcement. Namely that lives change, circumstances change. WHETHER WE WANT THEM TO OR NOT. When teenagers are braving the actual lived world of peers and family, classes and jobs and activities on a daily basis, as the months and years go by they come to see that they were never really stuck, that new always was in the process of coming, of replacing what was.

Teenagers grow up with no leadership about one's true self. We push them to be doers rather than beings. The Buddhists talk about mindfulness because that puts the person fully in the body, fully aware of the life and possibility around. Odd how our schools hold the sacred role of being second parents during the child's developing years, the years in which one learns to become an adult, yet these schools simply abet the direction of the popular culture.

I did a silly activity with an adult class that was seeking a grade 12 diploma. It was spring so I took them outside the classroom to a grassy hillside next to the building we were in. I separated them so they could be alone and then asked them to find a flower or plant that appealed to them and sit so they could look at it and pay attention, maybe talk to it in their minds, maybe just notice all the details and the energy of the plant they chose. There, all along this hillside were these adults of various ages sitting in silence and staring at plants and flowers! How nuts is that! Without a doubt it wasn't what they ever imagined they'd be doing in school that day. Then after ten minutes of silent sitting I had them come inside and write about the experience - what they saw, how they felt, why they chose the particular plant they chose, what they thought about the silence, any other thoughts that went through their minds, comparing the feelings and thoughts initially to the ones after several minutes had passed. After writing, we talked about it as a group. They all said they enjoyed the experience. But then later I got a note from the dean requesting I get a mental health examination. No, I'm kidding.

In high schools, silence is not valued for itself. It's insisted on solely to allow for instruction, reading, or tests to be conducted. Kids are not introduced to its importance. They aren't introduced to contemplation or stillness. I'll sometimes take my students out for walks during a class, but I'll set the rule that they have to walk by themselves and in silence. I ask them to pay attention to their surroundings and to their own inner processes. If I was asked, I'd call such exercises units in the curriculum of the self.

I went as a chaperone on a school trip to Thailand. What a wonderful destination for kids from the northern part of the globe. What an exotic place to visit. Culture, religion, geographical variation, pythons and elephants. The students were delightful to be with. They were keen, open eyed, and filled with joy at the new experience. Three weeks going from Bangkok to Chiang Mai and Chiang Rai in the north to Koh Phanang a paradisiacal island far in the south, they saw it all. They will remember the trip for the rest of their lives. Fifteen to eighteen year olds farther away from home then they had ever been in their young lives. This was real learning.

There was one discouragement for me, however. When we went on trains and busses to get from one city or region to the other, the kids did not look out the windows to watch the landscape. Instead they talked to each other, something they had ample time for every minute of the day and evening, or .....they put on their headphones and vegged to their music, in their own world. They had no interest or attention span for seeing outside. And there was lots to see, in some way a richer view of real Thai life then they were getting on the various tours we had arranged. We were leaving the Bangkok train station and for the first few miles we passed through slums and scenes of poverty right outside our windows. The group leader's wife started to cry out to the students to look out the windows. No one paid any attention. I tapped her on the shoulder and said, "It's no use. They don't care."

"But they should be seeing this. They need to learn how people live sometimes." I just smiled and told her that I agreed. I want to make it clear that this is typical teenager lifestyle, typical teenager behaviour. They don't care about what's out there at any given time. In their hearts they do. But in lived reality, as we allow them to live it, as we set them up to live it, they don't care because they don't understand. They have not been educated about "other". They have not been taught how to pay attention, how to be quiet and observe. Instead, they have become habituated in how to distract themselves, in how to disengage.

That Thailand trip was all about doing, experiencing and stimulation. It was wonderful and I'd take it any day as valuable education over what normally happens in schools. But the kids were not prepared to get the fullness out of it. Since that trip I've led several school trips to Prague and India. I tell the students before the trip that I won't allow use of headphones other than when they are in their hostels. I tell them about how the Thailand students missed out. I also do other preparation exercises that are designed to open the students to the deepest possible learning.

In our modern activity based lives, breathing is taken for granted. This fundamental component of our individual selves is not once examined or given attention. Breathing. Connected to silence and stillness; to say it is not on a school's radar is an understatement. In my counselling office, interaction is based on conversation. I encourage emotions to flow unedited. I encourage students to speak as freely as they wish. No need to censor language or stay in the normal etiquette of the school. Tell it the way it really is in your own chosen words. That's what I invite them to do.

But in many sessions, especially with those kids I've seen many times over, I'll have the student stop somewhere in the visit and just sit with me in silence. I'll ask them to put their hand on their stomach or chest and just slow down, breathe, and notice their breathing. We'll sit in silence for several minutes, just being together, two humans breathing, not kid and adult or student and counsellor but human and human. That's a healthy place to be for all kids, for all of us. A place to just be who we are. No good and bad, no positions of greater or lesser importance, no age even, just being self.

With various kids during various stages of therapy I might do guided visualizations. These all centre on breathing and attaining a relaxed state in which I try to slowly nudge the person into a state of self-love, self-acceptance. Teachers are often afraid to use such exercises in classrooms for fear of being branded as pushing religion or for fear that religious parents might object. Teachers are often afraid to try lots of things because of what parents or administrators will do. But visualizations and silent exercises don't need to have anything to do with religion. And rather than fearing the reactions of one, two, or even a few, so as to rob the many of experiences with their own calmest selves is a bad priority.

Whenever I teach creative writing I use visualization exercises and sometimes I even get the students doing a chant that I've made up in which they extend the tones with their breaths in order to hear a fascinating group sound. Then I ask them to write. Creative writing by definition is all about imagination. And exercises that stimulate imagination and produce fresh perspectives are integral to developing good writing.

In terms of being afraid of the reactions of principals, it's wrong to merely assert that teachers be fearless. I suggest that teachers maybe start slowly. Principals are responsible for what occurs in their schools. Introduce the least threatening activities first so as to get the principal acclimatized. The kids always enjoy the new and innovative. They're cool. Principals not so much. So the teacher needs to cultivate some trust and some anticipation with the principal. And they need to help the principal grow.

The single greatest learning experience that I ever had with my students was in a grade 8 social studies class when we were studying the Crusades. I quickly covered the historical aspects of what took place - King so and so, the Holy Land, the children's crusade, the Muslims, etc. etc. They'd all forget it so no need to labour the issue. But the concept of going on a crusade and getting passionate about a cause was something I wanted them to learn about and to connect with.

There is a truism about kids. They want to know about other kids more than anything else. Just watch how a tot responds to a new group of adults which includes another kid or even a teenager. The tot will look toward the young person first and most. Teens like to know how their peers think, and they respond to issues that affect other kids. I've often gained the absolute attention of classrooms of grade 12's by bringing in a "panel" of four grade threes or four grade eights and holding a talk show where I interview the panelists on various topics and then open it up for questions from the audience. I'll write more on this type of communion later.

For the Crusades unit, I separated the class of grade eights into groups of five and had them choose from the following topics, which they had to research and then report on to the class as a whole. I gave them one article on their topic in order to start them off. The topics were - child labor, female genital mutilation, illegal organ harvesting and female infanticide, street kids, child prostitution, child soldiers, the Young Offenders Act, and child slavery. All pretty serious and heavy topics, but all huge problems throughout our world today.

After each group had chosen an issue, done their research and presented to the class, they voted on the one issue that they all wanted to go on a "crusade" to do something about. They chose child prostitution. The "crusade" then entailed contacting an organization in a larger city nearby whose purpose was to work with prostitutes (including teens), to try and get them off the streets and into education. This organization, by chance, had just had its funding cut and was going to have to curtail some of its programs.

The class asked them if they could do some fund-raising. The head of the organization was astonished and quickly agreed. So the class went about setting up a display on child prostitution which they hosted in the school student center. They organized a raffle, a coin collection, and a bake sale. The media were contacted and we were on local radio and in the big city's newspaper. Two of the students had to get up at 6 A.M. to be interviewed for a morning radio program.

Letters and donations came in from people who, while driving to work, had heard the story on the radio. Everyone was taken by these twelve and thirteen year olds who were taking on the issue of child prostitution in their area.

But the part of the exercise that was most memorable for me was that the kids also asked if the head of the organization could come in to speak to the class and if she could bring in former teen prostitutes. When the principal found out he ordered me to stop it. Let the organizer come but not the prostitutes. I replied that since it was already set up that he should phone them and relay the alteration. Luckily he didn't, and so two days later they arrived to speak to the class.

There were three of them. Four actually. The woman in charge had brought two twenty year old girls and one of the girls had her baby in a stroller. For an hour, they sat at the front of the class, told their stories and took questions. The class learned how they had been recruited at the age of fifteen and sixteen. They learned about their home lives, the role that pimps and peer groups had played in their lives, and how they'd been off the street and clean for over six months, They learned about their pain and their shame. One of the girls cried during the presentation after the leader had acknowledged that this was her first time telling her story in public and how well she had done.

As the class ended and the students were leaving to join their buddies for lunch, I watched as one of the boys in class, a particularly rowdy and precocious fellow, met up with a pal just outside the doorway. The pal was looking inside the room and noticed the women, specifically the younger two, both quite pretty. "Who are they?" he asked.

My student said, "They used to be prostitutes." His friend's eyes got big and he started grinning, "Ooh, hookers!" he responded with glee.

My student didn't smile. He just said, "No, it's not like that. You don't understand."

I went back into the classroom knowing that the type of learning, which had just taken place, was rare indeed. These young teens had just had a crash course on humanity. Their hearts had been made wiser.

I later bumped into a very irate principal. He had discovered that the former prostitutes had been in his school and had talked to the kids. He was actually red in the face, feeling that we had agreed they would not come. I reminded him that we had also agreed that he would be the one to phone in that request. Later, when no negative phone calls came in from any of the parents of my students, he forgot about it.

Schools are so regimented and so rules oriented. Ask a student or teacher where they'll be on any given day and time in the future and they'll be able to tell you with fair certainty that they'll be in math class or in foods class. This is the case throughout the student's school life. Going outside the box is not expected. Schedules dictate everything.

That's why so many kids look forward to field trips. It doesn't matter where, just getting outside of the walls and the routines is enough to perk them up, make them look forward to the day. Nothing pushes the anticipation higher than a trip to a far away land. The Thailand trip in our school was always a big event. But it took place in the summer so school wasn't even in session. When I took students to India we went during the winter in order to have a favorable South Asian climate. That meant going a few days before Christmas break, all of the break, and a few days after. That meant being away from friends and family over Christmas.

It was also an expensive trip. This is one handicap and one regret about big trips in school. A certain section of the students will never be on those trips - the ones who can't afford to go or who believe that their economic reality is such that they don't even think about going. Yet each trip will include a couple of students who aren't getting any subsidy from their family, ones who are lucky enough to have jobs and who see the cost as being an investment in their own growth.

SHEILA - Sheila was one of those kids. She was a grade ten student when she signed up for the India trip. She was working twenty hours a week at a seniors care facility. She lived in a foster home because of serious problems with her family. The problems had been going on for years culminating in the parents turning against her. Sheila's parents had put the blame on her for, amongst other things, their own marital difficulties and went to Social Services to put her into foster care. Emotionally this kind of abandonment was very hard on Sheila. She knew herself to be quite alone and felt that deeply.

For some reason she was strongly attracted to going to India. I had billed it as a trip of a lifetime, one not for the faint of heart. It was a back-packers trip in which we would rely only on regular public transport - none of the charters of other school trips. We would be staying in budget accommodation and eating in the same facilities. The idea was to expose the students to the real India, a country where three hundred million live in dire poverty. I told the students that they were not going to have fun on the trip, that it was not a fun trip. They would be around extreme poverty and unfairness, live in conditions far less clean then what they were used to, possibly get sick, and in the case of the girls possibly get sexually harassed in one way or another. The learning, though, would be unparalleled.

Sheila had calculated that she could save enough from her earnings in the next seven months to go on the trip and she was keen to go. Every other student or their parents would drop off monthly cheques. Sheila would bring in an envelope of cash.

Two moments with Sheila on that trip are etched in me. One was when she and I were standing on a ledge beside the main cremation grounds in Varanasi, the holiest city of Hinduism and where devout Hindus all wish to die. We had wound our way through the narrow, ancient alleys to get to this site very near the riverside. Along our way, at least twice we had to squeeze to the side as chanting bearers came along with a corpse tightly wrapped in orange cloth at their shoulders on their way to the cremation *ghat*. The *ghats* are the great wide steps that descend at an angle to the holy Ganges River.

There are various *ghats* all along the Ganges as it courses through Varanasi from the Himalayas and on its way another thousand miles to the Bay of Bengal. They allow access for bathing, clothes washing, boat launching, and religious activities and ceremonies. The students had already arisen at dawn to be on a boat out on the river to observe the throngs of the pious up at sunrise to partake in their holy ablutions. And now much later in the afternoon, Sheila and I were at this ledge to have a closer look at the burning of bodies.

At this main *ghat* for cremations, the funeral pyres go twenty-four hours a day every day of the year. The logs for cremations are stacked in huge mounds. Members of the Dalit class, the untouchables, do this funeral work considered "unclean" to the orthodox Hindu. The man who owns the *ghat* is also a Dalit and is very wealthy. He's euphemistically called the king of Varanasi.

Before us were three funeral pyres ablaze and a fourth being readied. Mourning male relatives stood by each. The bright flames whooshed into the air. We could easily feel the heat from where we stood some eight metres from the nearest blaze. We stood in silence not knowing exactly what to think or how to feel about what we were witnessing and about ourselves doing the witnessing.

Should Hindu tourists come to our country and want to attend burials in our cemeteries we might consider it odd at best and more likely ghoulish. For sure we could consider the request insensitive and take some iota of offense. But there we were, Sheila and I, standing and watching intently with all of our mixed emotions. Watching the swathed body burn, watching the busy men laboring about it ensuring embers and burnt sticks went back into the flames. Farther away at other stations the workers raked at burnt debris, stroking through ashes to be gathered for ritual deposit in the holy water of the river. At the shore other workers were moving a wrapped body into a boat to be taken out into the river, weighted, and deposited to sink to the bottom. Such is the case that several types of people aren't allowed to be cremated - lepers, pregnant women, babies, and *sadhus* (wandering holy men) for example.

As we watched, Sheila calmly uttered, "Look, there's the person's bare leg and foot." Within the flames to the end of the pyre, a leg had come free from the swaddling and was burning before us as just another thin log. Together we pondered the meaning of all this, the meaning of what we were doing there and in India in general as these privileged Westerners who would return to their comfortable norms soon enough. Who were we to be gawking at someone's final earthly moments without a hint of connection or invitation?

It was not comfortable. It shouldn't have been. We both recognized that. We both opened up to the form of horror/cultural experience/voyeurism/lesson in truth and existence that we were beholding. We let it sink in. Later I gave her a long hug, as mutual as I've ever had with a student. We were a long way from home.

A week later we were in one of Mother Teresa's homes for the destitute in Calcutta. We had split the larger group into three more practically sized groups and for two days were volunteering in the various charitable sites operated by her order. Sheila was in the group I was with, and we were in a building for abandoned babies and children with significant physical and mental handicaps. These were the living dead, the ones who would be dead if not for the home set up for them by Mother Teresa. No one wanted them, but here they were wanted. They were given care, contact, and joy. An inscription on one of the walls read. "Beauty is perfected in deformity."

Our responsibilities were simple. Mingle. Visit. Feed those who needed feeding. Play. Help with laundry. I watched one of our students holding the tiniest of babies and feeding her with a small bottle of milk. I watched another walk around the rooftop terrace with a thin, angular blind boy of about ten years old. The boy was wound around him like a monkey as the student strolled about, talking and just being close. The blind child, who was also mentally challenged, of course, knew no English.

And a few feet away, I watched Sheila all by herself in a sleeping room filled with small cot after small cot. A little one had awakened from an afternoon sleep and was moaning. The child was very limited with cerebral palsy and seemed to be almost writhing in discomfort. Sheila had whispered to her that she wasn't the little girl's mother but just a friend, and she was stroking the little girl's hair. She began softly singing to her. So softly.

RHONDA - On a more humorous level, though still with earthy learning unlikely to ever be replicated in a classroom, one of our side trips in India took us to a small village where we visited a school. After we had gone to various classrooms to sing songs with the elementary level school kids, we took a short stroll through the village. We stopped to watch a potter making small clay cups for *chai*. We ambled between mud homes with cows chewing their cuds in the back. We swiped at flies as chickens squawked out of our way. Then we came to the end of the village and looked out into the farmers' fields.

I thought it an opportune time to have each of us walk out into the field and take a place twenty or so yards apart from each other just to sit in silence and feel the presence of rural India. The spirit of the land. The plots were dry, ploughed earth separated by low berms to divide it into large squares for different crops. It was almost overcast, so not as hot as it could have been. It was just right for ten to fifteen minutes of individual contemplation. This would be a small token to counter the many days of being always in smaller or larger groups, of being in cities, on the go, moving from visit to visit. Just us and the odd bird flying. Us and the field as ancient as civilization. Us and silence. Us and ourselves. Ahhh.

So there we all squatted or sat, scattered over this farmer's field. What passing Indians would have thought, who knows? I was enjoying the moments. Time passed. I scanned over the expanse to check that everyone seemed alone with their space. The warm felt good. The faintest of breezes felt good. We were in India on the other side of the world.

Then after the allotted time was up, I rose to my feet, gave a yell and a wave, and started to slowly walk back towards the road, carefully pacing atop the low berm divider. Others rose and did likewise. But after about forty feet I was coming up to Rhonda and she called out for me to halt. "Wait a minute, Mr. White. I think you should go around the other direction." What was wrong? I am afraid of snakes. Was it a snake? I noticed she was still squatting.

Then I heard another student cry out, "Aw yuck, Rhonda's going poo."

I belatedly noticed a bare butt bent appropriately and so I diligently went in the direction instructed. Afterwards, I heard some of the other girls critically discussing Rhonda's indiscretion. They were alluding to her free spirit nature but concluding that this time she had gone too far. On the walk to the cars, I made it a point to announce that Rhonda had been brave and wise. Since there were definitely no toilets to be had in the village, she had spared her trousers and spared the rest of us had she tried to hold it and failed. I'm not sure her peers were all convinced.

Ever the counsellor, I had Rhonda ride with me in the car I was in for the way back to the city and again praised her capacity to take care of herself and chuck western constraints out the window as necessity emerged. I patted her on the back and told her she was now a real traveller.

A week later, on the way back to our hotel from another side trip we were all riding merrily in the bus we had rented. It was dark out. Another girl came up to see me at the front. "Calvin, how much longer until we get to the hotel?"

"About 30 minutes, why?" I replied. We were already within the city limits but still far from the hotel.

There was a short pause, "Well, I don't think I can hold off until then. I have to poop. But if you give me a couple of those plastic bags and have everyone else move up to the front of the bus, I can just go in the back."

This was a girl whose mother had previously warned us was very sensitive about bodily functions, so much so that she was uncomfortable using the toilet in their own home while others were in an adjacent room. Clearly, Rhonda had started something.

As luck would have it, we were able to pull over a few minutes later to the side of the roadway where, after a few metres, a low stone wall cut off an empty scrub bush expanse. Out she got along with guess who ... Rhonda, of course. They went to places behind the wall to do their business. Other girls and one boy followed to do minor business. Yep, we had all arrived.

A light learning but in many ways a worthwhile one. Teenage girls in our culture have considerable barriers in regards to being au natural.

The travellers had been forced to let go - no pun intended - of restricting social conventions, and in so doing come to a bit more basic self-acceptance and the accompanying self-confidence.

This kind of exposure to truth and reality is how all of us advance, those who are undergoing the experience and thus those we later interact with. Going to such a faraway place as India is obviously not within the pale of most students and most schools. Most school districts would not be willing to risk the many uncertainties prevalent in such a trip. But the intimacy and the emotional challenge that such a trip affords can be looked for, albeit to lesser degrees, simply in the vision one sets for a classroom.

Recently, I substituted at another school in grade eight classes for a day. By chance the classes were studying India. I immediately started mulling over what I could do to provide them with something that might penetrate their routines and last in their minds for the future. I brought in some props: CD of Indian music, incense, batik of the Hindu god Vishnu, small wooden statue of the Buddha, and my anecdotes. But once in the school, I realized that it wasn't going to do the job. Since I was only going to have this one chance to give them a deeper peek, I needed something more.

Then I had an idea. Before the classes began I walked around the school looking for a small storage room with no windows that would be just large enough for 25 kids to sit wedged in on the floor and where there wouldn't be any light. And I found one. I went about setting up a make shift shrine with visuals, candle burning, incense glowing and the Vedic hymns playing on the CD player. I closed the door and went back to await the start of class.

I dropped down the wall map to show them exactly how far away India was from us and told them all that since they were studying India, it was necessary to go there to really get an understanding. Then I led them out of the classroom and down a couple of hallways into the closed and dark storage room. We all wedged into spaces on the floor. It was just big enough for everyone to sit, all touching arm to arm or feet to someone's backside in front of them. I asked them to not talk, and I explained how the small room we were in was the same size as the one that a friend of mine in India has lived in for forty years and in which, with his wife, he raised three sons. That was their whole dwelling except for a patio that extended on the front. For water and a latrine they had to share with the other families in the building in another area. I explained how Hindus of all statures worshipped at shrines often just as small as the one I had before them. That religion was very central and active in their lives. Then I just had them be quiet and listen to the music, smell the incense, and notice how the candle light flickered off the statue of the Buddha and the drape of Vishnu.

When a few minutes passed, I could see that they were allowing the experience in so I took the plunge and went further. These were very straight kids. I asked them if they wanted to hear a Hindu chant. They hesitatingly said yes. After a few rounds of me chanting the Hare Krishna mantra we all did it together. Then I led them in a few rounds of a Tibetan Buddhist chant. There in the dark on the floor in candle light and with incense wisping in the flickering shadows.

Afterwards I emphasized again that none of it was intended to convert them or suggest a religious preference, but merely to give them an experience outside their ken. I did the same routine with all four classes that day. For the final one, the teacher had returned and joined us. I could sense he was noticeably more ill at ease than any of the kids. Not because the exercise spooked him, but because it spooked him that the kids might tell their parents and say that he had also been a part of it. There were definite pockets of fundamentalist Christian homes in the community, and he feared repercussions. The day ended with one of the students asking if he could borrow the CD of Vedic chants.

Well, I know that it would be easy to get 200 people for a demonstration through facebook. The point is getting people who care enough to actually show up and take an interest. I think the problem isn't getting the message out there, it goes deeper than that. It involves getting people to actually care a little bit about social, environmental, ethical issues. I have yet to meet a 17 year old at school that I feel I can sit down with and just talk things out. They are either too emotionally self absorbed or they have shut down from feeling anything at all. It is sad, and I sometimes just want to give up and not bother anymore- people are so unwilling to see the bigger picture. I know that technology is one of the causes of this. We as teenagers have learned that it is so much easier to break up with somebody over facebook, to tell a friend you're mad at them through a text. We base our popularity on the number of "friends" we have accumulated on facebook. I used to hate it when my friends were on their cellphones in front of me; it made me feel like I wasn't good enough company for them. Now I think I've realized that they do it because they have no idea how to have a real conversation anymore. Texting is our language now.

And yes- I am certainly too busy. I won't argue that. I have, however, made a conscience decision to do less this year- no more advanced dance (which I hated, by the way), no more leadership, no more violin lessons. I realized last year that I am not the type of person who can handle doing EVERYTHING and still be a happy person. It took a while because my best friend is one of those people. I woke up this morning, I looked outside and all I wanted to do was go for a long walk, then come home and sit and watch the world go by. That is who I am- the real me. But she doesn't get to come out too often unfortunately.

On another note- I was wondering if you had any suggestions for some good books? I haven't had something good to read in a while and I am running out of ideas.

Letter From Kate – 17 years old

Kayla Fulton – 16 years old

Color Insert

Katie Crane – 17 years old *(See page xii)*

Stacey Malysh – 16 years old *(See page 57)*

Ellen – 14 years old *(See page 72)*

Misty – 13 years old *(See page 140)*

7. Kids Are Kids

Teachers are often so adamant when it comes to discipline and students. They espouse an ardent demand for accountability. "How will they learn otherwise?" "What message will it send to the rest if we don't...." and my favorite, "When they get out in the real world...." My suspicion is that what really infuses these sentiments is not the rationales that are trotted out but underlying unresolved issues in the teachers. The same phenomenon comes about with the clamors uttered about young offenders in our justice systems. "If they're old enough to do the crime then they're old enough to do the time"

A major attraction in teaching, albeit a hidden one, is the position of power it offers. The exercise of power. For sure, most of us were drawn to the profession because of more obvious reasons - wanting to make a difference in young lives, comfort in the world of the intellect, love of kids, the simple intrigue of accomplishing successful instruction, the money and holidays, etc. But beneath all of this we are all either consciously or unconsciously aware that we will also have regular power over others. Power to wield on a daily basis as we see fit. We know we get to be in charge. We get to be titled Mr. or Ms, or Mrs. or even better, Sir.

The wanting of power suggests a need for power. Usually a need for power stems from having been on the other end of it to detrimental results. I'm not trying to labor any big psychological theory here nor demean the calling of thousands and thousands of dedicated teachers, but simply pointing out that power is an element in the profession that is appreciated and sometimes coveted. When you see it in its uglier form is when emotions rise over disciplinary situations. It's the emotions rising that are the problem. The drive to get disciplinary results overrides the right decisions and right results for the kids. By right I mean that all discipline must have as its purpose the widest sense of well-being for the recipient. In other words we do discipline not for us but because it will genuinely help the recipient and genuinely respond to the needs of the situation and larger group.

It's long been asserted that with power comes responsibility. Living that responsibility means using discipline not to satisfy one's own impulses or emotional needs. It means assessing an incident, assessing the culprits and then responding in a way that will work towards the best outcome. The idea of punishment is something we need to graduate from. Accountability is also a tired concept. What works for the best outcome needs to replace both of those notions. But it's easy to fall back on aphorisms and buzz words. Especially if they fit with any emotional need for blood.

Remember Mr. Larson and the kid that told him to fuck off? Mr. Larson was angry, and his desire for discipline was driven by that anger, by the notion that he personally had been affronted, and that no one in his position of authority should be affronted in such a way. "No kid's going to get away with talking to me like that!" His personal emotions colored his conclusions for discipline. That's human nature. As professionals paid lots of money we have the responsibility to put discipline beyond that immediate and likely over-reactive gut reaction.

Punishment needs to be transformed into payment. A culprit needs to make payment for their transgression. Payment needs to fit the degree of transgression. Thus, someone who breaks a rule such as bringing alcohol or drugs to school probably needs to be kept away from the school. Possibly. It depends on who the kid is and what's going on in their lives, whether or not they already have a problem with attendance. For example, to suspend a kid who is already failing and who attends sporadically makes no sense. There are cases where a kid is just too far gone at the moment, too much of an incorrigible or negative influence on others that they should not be allowed in school period. But if the kid is his/her own worst enemy and not an overt danger or influence on others than we need to think of how to move him/her along, closer to pro-social and healthy behaviour. That means keeping him/her in school. That means coming up with a more creative but meaningful form of payment.

Payment also needs to be seen as legitimate in the eyes of victims. We might instinctively cry for punishment when we've been wronged, but with reflection and direction we can let that go and understand the justice which comes from adequate payment. That also is our job as educators - to reach the victims and help them refine and grow in their awareness of justice and consequences.

Schools rely on policy. They reach for their manuals every time there is a breach of the rules. It is rote and routine. There is no precision, no sensitivity to the needs, and no leadership in this approach to discipline. Disciplining for transgressions is an opportune time for learning. Schools botch it almost without fail. Instead of an organic, individual relationship and character-building event, it's made into a flat, mechanical interaction. Good riddance to the ones who we don't like and "I'm sorry but ..." for the ones we do.

School administrators and teachers use another aphorism to defend this methodology. Consistency. We must always be consistent. That's what policy ensures. We treat everyone fairly. This is a shallow understanding of consistency, and it undermines growth and leadership. Real leadership is when someone appraises the entire body of evidence and applies a response based on that evidence. That's the true meaning of consistency. Do it the same way each time, not do the same outcome each time. When Mr.Larson's detractor got a minimal consequence it was because a wise and fair administrator had seen the full picture.

Kids are not adults. By definition, it ought not to need even be stated. A Yogi Berraism. But we continually forget that when it comes to discipline, when they do something that makes us angry or pushes our buttons. The real world is full of allowances. Appointments are missed and rescheduled. Planes are held for passengers. Police hurt innocent people by mistake. Deadlines are extended. Contracts renegotiated. Yet I have seen teachers post a list of all the things that kids need to stop because the "real world" isn't like that.

In our wisdom we have made it non-binding for teenagers to sign contracts for goods or services until they are of age. They need parental signing for all sorts of undertakings. Medical procedures, purchases, marriage, passports, etc. There are laws that regulate employment and sexual interactions. Teenagers can't vote until they've reached a certain age. They can't join the military. All of this is because when we are sober in our thinking and not motivated by emotion or anger then we recognize that kids are indeed works in progress. They have not fully formed. They are not mature. They lack world experience, brain development, training, awareness, self-understanding, emotional development, and assertiveness. We recognize that kids can be easily manipulated, that they are vulnerable to authority and power to such a measure that there is an inordinate inequality and an unfairness to interactions with more authoritative adults. We recognize that they are more prone to emotional reactivity than an adult.

So, it is indefensible that we should ignore all this astute and accurate reasoning when kids commit transgressions. Even serious ones.

Even murder. Again I'm not saying that there needn't be adequate payment, adequate response, and adequate intervention. But I insist that it means an appropriateness to the reality of the offender's nature. A kid who commits a serious crime is not the same as an adult. A kid is still to go through huge changes and growth. An adult, not so much. If rehabilitation is a cornerstone of legal and justice precepts for adults than that same ethos should be dramatically magnified when it comes to kids. So much so that the idea of raising kids to adult court should never be an option. Never. Instead we need to redesign our laws for kids. We need to put more intellectual effort and money into designing innovative treatment programs that incorporate payment and transformative education and healing. Money ought not be an impediment.

Payment, indeed, might mean not having freedom for many years. Many years. But those years rather than being punitive, rather than being anger or vengeance based, need to be payment and building years. They need to be done in safe, productive, healthy confinement. This is all immensely doable. Schools can start the direction by redesigning their discipline policies to reflect a deeper understanding of consistency, accountability, and discipline.

A standard form of discipline for skipping classes is a suspension. A standard form of discipline for not doing schoolwork and homework is suspension. How logical is that? Causes are seldom sought. A teacher once told me with a straight face, "But what about those missing assignments?" I had just relayed to her information about a boy's home life. His mother had been suicidal. He was beside himself with worry and stress. I thought that knowing this the teacher would cut him some slack and figure out an alternative. Instead she nodded, shook her head in sympathy, and then blankly looked me in the eye and said what she said.

EARL - I learned a valuable lesson in one of the first years I was a teacher. I was teaching a grade 9 social studies class and I had a student named Earl who had failed the year before so he was repeating. I liked Earl and we got along quite cordially. I was a young teacher and it was important to me to be liked. I wanted my classes to be exciting and fun. In those days I stuck pretty close to the curriculum though I still experimented lots. I was charged up about being a teacher.

One morning Earl was being somewhat belligerent. He was talking to other kids during the lesson and being a distraction. When I intervened, he had been a bit snotty. Inside, I was shaken. My immediate feelings and thoughts were all about me. Oh, oh, Earl doesn't like me as much as I thought. Oh, oh I guess we don't get along so well. Oh, oh this class isn't going as well as I hoped and wanted to believe it was. They don't like me. All of this was going on inside me overtly and swiftly. All jumbled together. I considered my options. To blow up and send Earl out might risk losing the rest. They'd turn against me. Or the class would cease being an us and become a me and them. What to do?

Then for some reason I blurted something out. I can't say I knew what I was doing, certainly had not reasoned it out or understood it at all. It just came out and I know not from where, but it taught me and I've never forgotten the lesson. I said, "Geez Earl, are you having a bad day?"

Well, Earl's whole face shifted. He visibly relaxed, shook his head and said, "No, I'm having a crappy day. This morning...." and he went on to tell about how rocky his morning had been at home. I was astonished. The class didn't particularly react. No big deal. They hadn't been aware of any dynamic out of the ordinary. But Earl thenceforth was his old self again. There were no more distractions. I watched myself relax. The light bulb continues to shine in my head to this day. It's not about me. A kid's behaviour is not necessarily a comment about me or a threat to me. Discipline isn't necessarily needed. Understanding and clarity are. And personalizing doesn't help.

This was long ago; I never had any dealings with Earl after the course finished, never got closer to him or maintained the relationship. I left the school the next year. But Earl's face back there in the end few seats of row two is indelibly in my mind's eye. It's not about the teacher, it's about the student.

I feel as I should
even though I say
constantly
we choose
I am not so
sure
anymore.

I am sure
I have a bellybutton

I have constant female
companionship
girls tend to love me
whether its like a brother or not
they have always been available
when my mum
left
I was hurt
I honestly feel
like I chose
that hurt, but I didn't
I beat myself up
I have to be honest with
myself
we have choices
but they're not all
made by
"you".

Chris – 15 years old

What really affected me was the part of the children. How they stayed up all night, they could hear everything. I know I was one of those children. Maybe that's why I am the way I am. Strong, witty, and can keep things together on the outside, but not on the inside. Because I saw my mother defend herself, her children, and try to make it look to everyone else that her life is perfect, when in fact it wasn't.

I remember that at least four or five times a month my parents fighting. I remember this from as young as the time O could climb out of my crib. Some nights I would go into my own little world and play with my Barbie. Just lay in my bed, she had this beautiful dress and I pretended she was in a fashion show o she was a singer. Once I remember my mom just standing in the dor of my room watching me with tears in her eyes.

I've walked out of my room and found her laying on the floor unconscious. We ended up leaving her there. My dad took us to his parents house and kept calling her. When she finally answered he let me talk to her. She was crying. All I kept saying was are you all right mommy? She just kept telling me, I'm fine sweetie, I'm fine.

Now for me to watch something like this video and see myself as a statistic and I wonder to myself was I the only child in my family to witness this and remember or did my brother as well, or was he too young?

I feel a sickness in my stomach to think my mom went through all she did all on account of love for her children and the fear of being alone.

Karine – 16 years old after watching a video on spousal abuse

Misty – 13 years old *(See page 132 Colour Insert)*

8. Boys Will Be Boys?

Much hand wringing and expression of consternation has recently emerged over the growing academic gap between the genders in Canadian schools. Boys are falling behind girls in both performance and enrolment in the senior academic areas of not only literature, geography, and history, but also the more traditional strongholds of math and sciences. We lament this because we care about the future for the boys. But there is a far more troubling gender gap which has emerged, one with a greater consequence than just the limitation of boys' futures. A gap that is more akin to canaries dying in the coal mine.

Within our high schools, the areas of leadership, social responsibility, and activist contribution to community are hugely dominated by females. In high schools offering leadership classes, girls are in the ever-growing majority. One can assume this is because boys no longer resonate with the notion of being leaders.

In the past seven years I have led three school district trips to India. These trips were demanding forays intended to challenge the personal resources of the students as they were thrust into various scenarios far outside their comfort zones. Students were told the trips would not be fun, but that they would leave them glad for the experience and feeling wiser and more confident. The poster said it would be the hardest trip they ever made. Of nineteen students on the first trip, three were boys. On the second trip there were five boys out of nineteen. The third trip consisted of eleven students and only one was a male. This was a surprising disinterest in an exciting emotional and physical challenge.

I have also led six school trips to Prague and central Europe. That itinerary is filled with cultural experiences – jazz, symphony, opera, smoky clubs, Premier league hockey and soccer games, galleries, castles, Jewish internment sites, and lots of free time for exploring. These trips also have all had a ratio of two thirds female and one third male.

These examples can rightly be criticized as anecdotal and not particularly convincing. However, there is more compelling evidence. The Canadian NGO, Free The Children, annually stages a major event called WE DAY in several of Canada's largest cities. These WE DAYs involve bringing in high profile speakers and entertainers as part of a spectacle intended to inspire Canadian students to become community and globally involved in bringing about positive change. The idea is to engage our youth with the concepts of social justice and human rights, particularly as they affect children. In some respects, it's an attempt to build global leaders, to encourage and offer opportunities for youth to shape their world. And as important, to instill the idea that they, as individuals, have the power to bring about positive change.

WE DAYs are major youth events, unprecedented in their star power. In 2009, speakers included the Dalai Lama, Robert Kennedy Jr., and Jane Goodall plus performer Justin Bieber. In 2010, it was Al Gore, Jesse Jackson, and Martin Sheen. 2011 brought Mikhail Gorbachev, Mia Farrow, and Shaquille O'Neal. The big names are rounded out with various other inspirational speakers and captivating big name entertainers. It's all a magnetic pulse of energy and significance. In Vancouver, for instance, 18,000 students from all over B.C. and some parts of Alberta filled GM Place for 2012's line-up that included Desmond Tutu, Magic Johnson, and the band OneRepublic. Schools choose the attending students on the basis of some kind of contributing to others. The school district from my area sent seven busses of 400 kids the five hundred kilometres to Vancouver. Astoundingly the ratio of girls to boys was 9 to 1. It was obvious that the ratio of the full 18,000 was no better than 4 to 1.

At the media session with Free The Children founder Craig Kielburger, I asked for his take on the gender disparity. He nodded his head and responded that of the hundreds of volunteers each WE DAY uses, 70 to 80% are female. The same ratio holds true for those who do summer internships or take part in summer programs that Free The Children operate. He said that was one reason for bringing in NBA stars Shaquille O'Neal and Magic Johnson - an attempt to appeal to more boys. It obviously hadn't worked.

So, what does it mean and what's the big deal? We seem to be producing generations of males who either do not see themselves as fundamental to the growth and well-being of their communities and planet or who lack the desire, confidence, or will to take their place in responsibility and leadership. Both scenarios are scary. This is especially so when considering what does draw the male resonance. In Toronto, in April 2011, 55,000 spectators snatched up tickets for an Ultimate Fighting Championship event. Mixed martial arts is the fastest growing "sport" today. I think it can be safely assumed that the vast majority of the 55,000 were men.

Since the 1960's, women's lives have surged forward with an expanding of how they see themselves, what they expect for themselves. Women's world view and self view continue to open and grow. This has not been the case for men. Their world view, if anything, has atrophied. Young girls are moving into a future where they only see possibilities and "can do". Young boys look forward and wonder "what now?". Boys do not know who they are or what it means to be male. Schools don't engage them in that conversation.

And now with the total immersion in technology, everyone is channeled into more insularity in terms of their gaze. We look into our text pads, our video games, and into our computer screens. Compared to any other time in human history, we no longer look directly out to our environment or to our others.

If this direction continues, males will inevitably find themselves in such a squeezed reality that there will be predictable consequences which run from sad but benign to sad but frightening.

"We are destroying our boys." I recently put that to classes of grade 9's and grade 12's. Their response shocked and saddened me. They agreed. Until I actually voiced it to kids, the notion had only been my own derivation. The un-coached confirmation and then, more specifically, the perceptible unease in the eyes of the boys sitting in those classes hit me like a dart. I'm not talking about a physical destruction, but a character destruction, an atrophying of identity.

Kids grow, but they do not grow in a vacuum. They grow according to the nourishment they receive or do not receive and according to the directions presented for their growth. Schools are a key component of that, maybe the decisive one. These are the wireless times, a step further along the vortex of electronic gadget dominance. The innocent days of kids gathered around a Mario Brothers or Sonic Hedgehog quest on a TV screen have morphed to a lone child immersed before the credit card sized screen in his palm.

This is a megaton shift away from being connected to the complex pulse of the external, real world of human interaction and all of which that consists: world affairs, social activism, negotiating through interpersonal conflicts, nuancing communications, local community needs, and on and on. Despite the electronic opportunities for connectedness, which have been especially productive in the developing and repressive parts of the planet, this new form of technological immersion tends to insulate and isolate. Our young look inward rather than outward. Narrow their vision rather than expand it, (YouTube notwithstanding). And dull and trivialize their purview.

In any given classroom that has computers, allow students free time and they inevitably flock to cyber junk food. A recent draw in one classroom that I was in was the clip purporting to show professional wrestler Brock Leznar snapping the arm of a nemesis. The students were intent on determining whether or not it was true or fake.

Though both genders are suffocated in this mess, the girls have been thrown a crucial lifeline while the boys have been left to sink. They seem happy enough in that sinking. Until, that is, it's put to them that they are being destroyed, and then it becomes clear that at a more internal level they are all too aware of their predicament.

The girls' lifeline has been developing for decades now. The birth control pill, women's lib, feminism, magazines tailored to expand and motivate their full potential, sports leagues for women, female super heroes and action figures, and a continuous theme of reaching out to and cultivating the capacity for female greatness. Girl power, Oprah, Madonna and Lady Gaga, you name it there has been an ongoing promotion of female rights and the presumption of success.

Programs and initiatives designed to bring more girls into the trades, into politics and government, and into other traditional male bastions all combine with the aforementioned phenomena to open a channel for girls to flow into meaningful and rewarding futures. Futures in which the sky is the limit and that the latest generations of females automatically assume as natural to them. Their names as females have been called.

And when was the last time you heard the term "boy power"? The last time you saw a promotion for anything positive that explicitly focussed on boys?

What we do have are movies and activities that implicitly call to boys and these inevitably revolve around violence or toughness or triviality. Military recruiting ads, mixed martial arts and its "ground and pound" mentality, pornography with its male dominance, video games that blast and destroy, and sports team camaraderie. Our boys take their role models from the scripted stars of athleticism complete with their "bling" and bravado or false humility. They watch themselves in the superficial world of movie one-liners and buddy road trips. No wonder booze and drugs have such an allure for male teenagers!

Where do they get a sense that meaning, depth, worthiness, complexity will be the character of their future? We are told that in a couple of decades the vast majority of lawyers and doctors will be women. This is not to suggest at all that we need to stop any initiatives or encouragements for women, but that we need to target boys now specifically as boys. We need to promote and directly teach/train to ideals of importance other than those oriented to physical power. And not simply in the area of computer and software design. We need to create a lifeline for boys that points toward leadership, holistic communication, intellectual challenge, compassionate engagement with others, and multi-faceted success. Schools need to emphasize global and self-awareness, teamwork, confidence development, resourcefulness, perseverance, and involvement FOR BOYS.

In other words, and simply put, our boys need help and they need help now or else we will have generations of lost and floundering adult males. Just ask the boys what they see up ahead.

9. The Substance In Substances

There are logical reasons why kids get into drinking and drugging. It's not a sign of stupidity. It's more a sign of someone's survival instincts. Getting high feels good. That's the key to any intervention program. Sadly, most of the time it is totally ignored. SAY NO TO DRUGS! Bring in the police or the experts to scare, lecture or talk the kids out of the bad stuff. Marijuana is a gateway drug, right?

We're all mixed up, and we're part of a big lie. Adults everywhere are drinking to excess on a regular basis. Adults everywhere are getting high on marijuana on a regular basis. Government makes money from it. Movies joke about it. Celebrities smile about it. And Uncle Jim reeks of it every so often when he's over for a visit. Adults do it because it makes them feel good, because they like it. Kids are the same. Why should they say no when adults don't? If it's so bad and so scary, then why is it so prevalent? Kids can figure it out at a very young age.

By implementing the superficial anti-substance abuse programs that we currently use, we only once again indicate our own duplicity, confusion, and lack of trustworthiness to teenagers. The pulpit long ago lost its effectiveness. Kids can access their own facts on the internet. We can't scare them with misinformation. Authority has no clout in terms of convincing or persuasion.

Kids teach us everything we need to know about influencing substance usage. Books and authorities are usually disconnected. I was working with this particular group of grade 10 boys that I was close to, trying to get them to cut down on their marijuana smoking. I know that, regardless of what any pot proponent says, marijuana use by developing minds retards that development. It falsely trains them how to solve problems and it falsely trains them how to feel good. It takes them away from the self they awake to each morning so that self has less chance of growing strong and resourceful in its evolving. It interferes with their capacity to think with acuity, duration, and complexity when they're in school.

Thus putting another impediment in the way of acquiring those skills. And because a marijuana high layers the consciousness, creates an altered state, it reduces the opportunities for genuine unfiltered intimacy.

I was making limited headway with the boys. Even though we got along very well and there was a great deal of trust, I was finding it hard to effect any great change in their habits. As with drinking alcohol the social aspect of marijuana use is very alluring. Then one day just before the final bell, one of the boys stepped in to my office to tell me of his progress with a certain girl and that he had done lots of school work that day. He finished off by saying he was looking forward to getting home and lighting up a joint.

That's when I got it. I knew all about the more intricate pulls and underpinnings of marijuana usage, but until that moment I had not understood what was really happening and where I was going wrong. The boy was telling me he was looking forward to getting high to put the final touches on his good day. In my work with these kids, I was trying to take something away that each of them really looked forward to. I was trying to take away what gave them camaraderie and happiness. Of course they were resisting that. They all wanted to please me. They all valued and enjoyed my interest and involvement with them. They liked the no bullshit honesty we shared. So, it was a strain for them to have to resist me. But I was trying to take something away and wasn't replacing it with something equally effective.

When that boy left to catch his bus home, I was in "hmmm" mode. I finally understood what I was up against. All the information, all the reasoning, the cultivating of a strong relationship, the exploration of when, where, why, and how those boys used marijuana, the counselling was not going to work. It might seed something for the future and undoubtedly was giving them something, but it was not going to change their immediate habits. At best it would alter their practice of smoking up during school hours.

We live in an age of addiction. Governments abet the proliferation of casinos and lotteries to reap the tax benefits, all the while knowing that the backbone of the industry is people's hopes and dreams for a better life and their proclivity for excess, their inability to control impulses. Liquor is advertised and sold in as many outlets as possible. Consumerism and material acquisition is the true religion of our times in the West. We have to buy things.

Kids don't see why what they use for release or for fun is bad and what everyone else uses is okay. So, in a nutshell, I don't think we can stop drug and alcohol usage by our young. What we sow, we reap. This is amplified obviously when a kid's own parents are serious users.

HARMON - Harmon was a fresh faced grade eight boy when I first met him. I had a group of kids outside in a field sitting in a circle in the sunshine. We were getting to know each other. I brought up the idea of physical punishment from parents. Being hit. We talked about it for a few minutes with Harmon being noticeably vocal. Then he added, "Actually, I find mental or emotional punishment worse than getting hit." We all looked at him. He explained that when a parent was really angry or really cutting in their comments those words were more painful for him than most blows. Hurt feelings outweighed hurt flesh. He talked about how small and helpless it made him feel and how lasting it could be, whereas when he had been physically hit, he had forgotten about it the next day.

I think everyone was shocked at the candor and openness. He was also a bit of a rough and tumble kid. No one expected the eloquent insight. As the months and years went, by Harmon and I had many private discussions about his childhood and life. His estranged father was in another city some distance away. Harmon had initiated contact, but the dad was only marginally interested. That hurt. But he had a good relationship with his mother and half-brother and half-sister, all three of the kids with different fathers. Harmon was the middle child.

Harmon was also seriously addicted to marijuana. He smoked every morning before school, during school, and in the evening at home in order to go to sleep. Already he had been suspended from school for a marijuana transgression. It was not uncommon to smell it on his clothing, and after lunch break his eyes would have that glaze. He was such an honest kid, when the vice-principal had called him in and confronted him, he admitted it right away. He had been sent home for ten days. A second transgression would mean losing the entire semester.

I saw my job as influencing Harmon away from dependence on the high. Of all the dope smokers I have known over the years, Harmon was the most honest and the most open. He knew, and I soon recognized, that he was also fully addicted. This was nothing he could change. Often when I work with dope smokers or drinkers I will challenge them to investigate whether or not they are addicted, whether or not they use by choice or compulsion. Everyone I have ever worked with always claimed it was from choice. So, I ask them to investigate, to check it out. We agree on going one week without drinking or doing the drug. Just to see if the kid can do it. I emphasize that it's up to the kid, that he or she is trying the experiment out of free will, that it isn't to placate me. Once we agree to this, we wait out the week. Every kid comes in after that week to boast that, "See, I did it."

I respond that then they can go ahead and use it that weekend if they want, that the first trial is finished. But I ask if we can visit again the following week. During that week I negotiate another abstaining period just to see. We agree to a month. I explain that addiction would likely flare its head before a month, that if the kid could go a month by choice then there's a good chance that they weren't actually addicted, merely enjoying it as they claimed. If they won't try a month - don't want to miss out on all that fun and camaraderie - then I'll go for two or three weeks. Whatever I can get.

Part of this is to genuinely join with them in the discovery of how deeply they are connected to the substance use. The other part is to practise restraint and choice making, to give them practical experience with self-discipline. It's also intended to give their developing psyches a chance to be substance free for a time. And it's a connecting activity between counsellor and client. It builds trust. I'll come back to this in a bit.

When I put my challenge to Harmon he just laughed and said that there was no way he could go even three days without weed. "I know I'm addicted," he matter of factly stated. He would rather he wasn't but, as he saw it, there were worse things. He knew it caused him limitations in his studies. Completing assignments was very difficult for him. Staying on track in class was difficult. He was a boy that needed to move about, at least a little bit every few minutes just to keep himself engaged. His home life was beset with no money. His single parent mom lived from paycheck to paycheck when she was able to sustain a job.

They lived in a neighbouring smaller town in which there were literally no organized activities for teenagers. Kids from that town could go for walks or they could stay at home and watch television. Teenagers need more than that. This is no idealized world where kids "should invent their own fun, like we used to have to do." Teenagers in Harmon's town smoked dope or drank for their leisure stimulation. If they had the resources then they got driven back and forth from their home to my town where the school was for the various activities and teams offered there.

That was not possible for Harmon. They had a car but no money for any kind of regular trips. Over one Christmas holiday, I bought Harmon and his older half-brother snowboard lesson/rental day passes. They had never been on a ski hill. Their mom agreed she could get them there. They were extremely appreciative. The older boy, whom I didn't know well, came in to shake my hand, uncertain of how he should feel about the unexpected gesture but grateful nonetheless.

Harmon knew and felt his life to be boring and dull. He loved his family but getting through each day and with memories of a missing father, of being hit by a former stepfather, of watching his mother be hit, he needed help to feel okay each day. He needed to create his own reality. Marijuana did that. His mother knew how much he smoked and urged him to cut down. She felt bad about it, but sometimes she and Harmon would smoke up together.

I counselled with Harmon from a to z. We covered all the traumas, did all the information. It was enjoyable to Harmon and I got him to cease doing marijuana during school hours. Most of the time. He started a love relationship with a girl in a higher grade. She didn't smoke dope so that was the bigger help. It was clear to me that I wouldn't be getting any further. As he grew and life circumstances changed, I hoped he would be able to make other changes. I did do one other thing for him though. It was unprofessional and certainly unorthodox.

I saw Harmon as a very positive boy. There was no meanness or negativity in him. Life circumstances were not in his favour at the moment. He had become addicted at a young age. It should be stated here that at the time there were no residential treatment centres for teenagers. That has hardly changed to date. We are so out of touch with our responses to drug and alcohol abuse. Harmon was addicted but it was not hurting anyone but himself. School was a positive place for him. As long as he was at school there was hope. I could continue my connection. He would be with peers. His life would have sociability. And he would pass some courses. So, I told him to lie if he ever got accused of smoking dope at school again. I told him that unless they catch him with the marijuana in his hand or locker, that they can't fully prove anything. I almost ordered him to lie.

In my career, I've had very good and very close relations with administrators. By the luck of the draw, almost every one of them was intelligent, aware, flexible, and kid centred caring people. But they have a school to run and a responsibility for order and rules. I'd normally be abetting that to the best of my ability. But in Harmon's case, I concluded that he needed an ally. He needed someone who understood and who could see the bigger picture. The school was not going to be put in the worse if Harmon never got caught again. They could catch others. He wasn't going to be any influence on anyone else. Typically, teenagers are already so familiar with marijuana, no one kid has any noticeable negative influence.

So, I explained to him why I wanted him to lie. "Don't smoke at school, but if you do and they bring you in, then deny it. Unless you have some on you, they can't actually prove you were using. Being in school will serve you better than being stuck at home. You are sick, addicted. I don't want that being the reason for you being penalized. School is giving you positive experience and contributing to you growing." My role is to act and think in terms of what is the greatest good for the kid, not what the rules are.

In this regard, it is also how I work with all the kids who are using alcohol or drugs. That is, my primary goal is to develop an honest relationship with them, to give them the experience of being in an honest relationship with a thinking, caring adult to whom they owe nothing.

As part of our school's substance abuse response, I decided to organize an assembly for the two youngest grades. I gathered together a group of four students each of whom I knew had different habits of usage. Teenagers have heard it all. Authorities have lectured, postered, audio-visualled, and disciplined ad nauseum. I don't see substance abuse down. So, I thought I'd try kids talking to kids.

CURTIS, FRANCINE, KALVIN, AND JANIE - I did order how the four would present to the group, and I chose the one who would introduce the others. Janie started by explaining that the purpose of the assembly was to offer opinions and experiences about marijuana use but not to try to convince anyone of anything. Instead it was to get them to think. To make their own minds up.

First was Curtis. He related how he used to smoke marijuana all the time, telling them when and how he had first been introduced to the weed. He told everyone how it made him feel and how it eventually started to affect him. Rather than sustain the pleasant relaxed sensations, he had found his toking up to have dulled him. He no longer liked the feeling and so had cut down drastically so that he now only smoked less than once a month if that.

Then came Francine. She had only smoked marijuana a few times. She spoke of how her sister was a user but that she had chosen not to go that route. Again, she began by relating her first experience and what had made her start, who she had been with, what it had all been like.

Francine hadn't smoked marijuana for two years and had no plans to continue. It just didn't do anything for her and she felt that it had screwed her sister up, causing her to fail at school and trigger family discord.

Next came Kalvin. Kalvin had a big grin on his face. He immediately told everyone that he loved marijuana and liked to smoke it as often as he could. The assembled students went wild, hooting and laughing. Kalvin kept talking. He explained how and when he had first tried it. He explained all the feelings that it gave him and why he liked those feelings. Again everyone hooted. But then his smile dropped and he realized that people weren't listening closely enough. He mentioned that he believed he needed to cut down. His grades were too low. He told everyone how he had been suspended for smoking at school, that the next time he got caught he would lose the year. So, he said, he no longer smoked at school. He now thought that doing that was stupid and not in his best interest. School, he said, should be a place where you tried to achieve something. He had come to the conclusion that risking suspension was dumb and that fogging his mind during school hours was dumb. The assembly was much quieter now. Kalvin finished by again saying that he knew he should cut down but that it was hard and he likely wouldn't. His last words were that he thought it would have been better for him if he had never started in the first place, but that he didn't think it was all so terrible what he was doing.

During this assembly, the vice-principal was sitting beside me. He was physically squirming. Because Janie had began by saying that no adult was going to talk, that this was students talking to students, he knew he couldn't jump in no matter how concerned he was. It was too late. He had only then realized how free and open it was going to be. I can still hear his sighs and see his teeth clenching.

Last to speak was Janie. Hers was a different story. Janie had never smoked marijuana. She talked about having values and that her values were not to do anything that would lower her esteem in her own eyes. She admitted that almost all of her crowd, the friends she hung out with and cared about, all smoked marijuana and used other drugs. She stayed committed to her own standards. She talked about standards and what she wanted for her life. She finished by again saying that she didn't want any-one to think she was trying to tell them what to do. The whole purpose of her story and the stories of the other three were to open up the subject and to stimulate thought. "You all have to make your own minds up. That's the point...to think and make your own minds up."

They took some questions. Then Janie dismissed the students and that assembly was over. The principal had come in early into the presentation. He had been standing in the back. I approached him. He had a serious look on his face. All he said was, "We'll be hearing about this from parents." I knew he wasn't happy with it or with me for setting it up.

Of course, there never was one phone call. The students all knew it had been a rare experience. No adults. No message trying to sway them. Just the message to think. They had never heard such uncontrolled candor before at a school offering. All four of those kids who presented got a lot of positive feedback. Even the principal begrudgingly gave Kalvin a pat on the back the next day when it started to don on him that there would be no ill repercussions from parents. He understood that the message had been in the right direction and that it had been beneficial. He understood the power of letting the kids take the leadership.

It was a bit of a setup on my part because I had known the kids and they had all understood that we really did want kids to not become dope smokers. Even Kalvin didn't want them to. But they all knew that trying to change people's minds, preach or tell them what to do would not work nor was it what they wanted to be doing. All agreed that the right route was to get people thinking rather than following or fitting in. They knew how easy it was to be mindless. They knew that no one had ever gotten them to really think about it.

The assembly had been an incredible experience of trusting kids. It had scared me too. I had seldom let go of the reins like that. I didn't know how it would turn out, didn't know what the four would exactly say or how they would say it. I did know I wanted Janie to close it off so as to leave her example as the last one in their minds. But more importantly I wanted the assembled juniors to be modeling from their peers - modeling thoughtfulness, forthrightness, leadership, personal decision-making, and engagement with the idea of using marijuana, engagement with the idea of reflecting on their own well-being, values, growth, and courage. And Kalvin became a leader that day. He learned. Overall, the respect quotient in our school rose noticeably from that assembly.

Contrast this with other substance education assemblies or school visits. Usually, it's bring in a play, trot out the dusty two hour unit on the variety of street drugs, and assemble the student body for a counter-attack speaker with sobering message - no pun intended. Frequently, the school or district will have a designated counselor for substance related issues. Mission accomplished - the education authorities can claim to be on top of the need to tackle the drugs and alcohol issue. Of course, the police will also have some involvement.

The police? They're the ones that the good guys rely on to protect them from the bad guys. The ones teens try to get away from when they are having a party. They carry guns, Tazers, cuffs and billy clubs. Bullet-proof vests. Media features or commentary on illicit drugs always include police spokespersons telling of the prevalence, dangers, and advisements. Schools liaison with officers to do drug presentations at both elementary and secondary levels. Thus, the underlying message intended or otherwise is a moral one and a legal one. Drugs are morally bad and don't break the law.

Over the past few years we've charted and highlighted the risks of successively emerging scourges - crack cocaine, PCP, ecstasy, crystal meth, and now "bath salts" and Oxycodone. And we rely on the message of morality and legality issued by police. The symbol of authority scaring kids. Warning them. Lecturing them. Uniforms in the classrooms.

How is this received by the captive audience? Well, for starters it puts pre-teens in an awkward emotional place of denial, resistance, or confusion. Inevitably, marijuana is included as one of the bad drugs. It's routinely termed a gateway drug to the "really bad drugs". In Canada there is a marijuana political party, several American states have now voted to decriminalize it, 4/20 is celebrated across the country, celebrities galore partake, and many kids know their own parents or siblings smoke dope. Police finger wagging about marijuana, at best stretches credibility and, at worst, instills a conflict of shame and loyalty.

When it comes to teenagers, credibility is everything. Any message about their lives and their choices will be quickly tuned out if the messenger isn't credible or the message doesn't ring true. In the last five years, all of Canada has learned that police officers Tazered to death a Polish immigrant at the Vancouver International Airport and lied about the facts, that police bungling in the investigation of the serial killing of women in the British Columbia lower mainland allowed more victims to fall prey, that police officers don't always follow the rules when they shoot to kill, that they drink and drive and kill people when doing so and try their best to lie their way out of it, and that they belong to forces rampant with sexual harassment. The list goes on. These are the credible "teachers" about drug dangers?

I once did presentations on crystal meth to groups of two hundred teenagers. I started by passing around a pizza box with a fresh cow pie in it. After the ensuing cries of disgust and laughter died down, I suggested that none of them would dip their fingers in and start chowing down if they were told they'd get a great high from doing so. Then I brought out all the ingredients that go into producing crystal meth. I showed photos of the protective suits the cops wear when they take down a meth lab. I talked about how that drug is marketed, why it exists, how the catchy name is even manipulative, and how kids are being tricked and used when they take it. Then I passed the microphone over to the real expert.

She was the mom of the biggest dealer in the region. The 24 year old was now "retired", but had been a heavy user of crystal meth. For more than half an hour there was total silence other than her voice. She talked about the nightmare she and her son had lived through for three years. Near death experiences, hospitalizations, recurrent hallucinations, constant edginess. She showed his teen photos and his current photo. A really nice looking kid. We had planned to have him do the presentation, but he had needed to move to another town to start a job. His emotional state was still shaky, and neither he nor his mom wanted to add strain by having him postpone the job move. At the close, the mom took questions. Then kids lined up to give her a hug. Later in the day, at various times, kids randomly came up to me and thanked me for the assembly. I knew it was because I had the sense to connect them to someone they could trust.

They had all been moved. They had all listened. This could have been their mom. She did not preach, didn't try to convince in any way. She just told them what happened. Human to human. The credibility of experience, authenticity, and sameness. She was them. I am convinced that a similar outcome would have occurred if her son had done the presentation.

To reach kids, to prompt them to think and to choose wisely, it's necessary to get inside their walls, to gain a relationship, to have trust. They trusted the mom, and they would have trusted her son. There was zero moralizing and zero legalizing. Rather than scaring there was sharing, revealing the pain. To reach kids we need to bring in other kids and other moms, former young users and dealers who can share the lived truth. Let the real experts talk, and let the cops stick with catching bad guys.

Drinking and driving has been a part of my life since I was born. My father is a hardcore alcoholic. Everytime he drinks he wants to drive. I can remember when I was twelve, my dad was way too drunk to drive so, I took matters into my own hands and drove all the way from Amherst to Lowen. (35 miles) My mother says my dad has been drinking and driving all of his life, therefore he's good at it. Well, obviously he's not, he has something like twenty-four drinking and driving charges and he just got his license back this year. I went to dinner with my dad and my brother for my brother's 19th birthday on April 5th. Everybody was so drunk after they came out of the bar and I noticed my dad going straight for the car door. This is when I began to realize that drinking and driving is sort of a habit. Needless to say I drove the car home instead of the drunks.

Phillip – 16 years old

10. Bully For You

L et's look at how we approach the problem of gangs. In any socially or ethnically mixed school environment there is a potential for tribalism and for the acting out of pain. Misery enjoys numbers. Numbers mean power to get what you want. This may be what you don't have enough of or it's straight acting out, releasing the trauma already suffered. Police, punishment, and discipline are a needed component in tackling gangs. But they won't change anything.

Schools, because of the mass of time that kids spend there as they develop, are where gang involvement needs to be addressed. The foundation principle and intention for schools must be to know the kids. We start by learning about them, about what they've experienced, what they live with, how they see life. Then we build relationships. Every teacher should be assigned a group of kids that becomes their "family" until the kids graduate. The teacher needs to become the mentor, the involved adult.

When we know our kids, we have a chance to influence their choices. When healthy adults have sustained relationships with kids, we have a good chance to influence their choices. Sometimes the kids will still go the wrong direction but they'll go that way with an inner experience of having had someone care about them, of having been respected and listened to, of having had value. These factors greatly soften the intensity and duration of negative choices. They're like a hook to the other pro-social world.

Obviously, teachers and schools cannot change the whole social reality of neighbourhoods and communities. There are no answers or easy solutions to complex realities, but there are concrete measures that can be enacted which will have significant results. We need to clue in to the latent power that we've always had and shift our mindset. To educate does not mean to instruct or to assign grades. It means to develop the whole being.

Gangs offer belonging, power, status, and material gain. Who doesn't want some of that? Sometimes kids join gangs because they're afraid not to. Who doesn't respond out of fear? Other times kids join because their futures seem hopeless otherwise so why not go out with a bang, no pun intended. Does that also not seem to make sense?

Positive relationships, positive peer networks, stimulating physical, intellectual, and emotional activities on a regular basis, and basic physical safety are the ingredients to strive for that will have the greatest effect on gangs. Schools can provide each of these if that is their intent.

The other strategy that will bring about change is to pay attention to the gang leaders. Instead of demonizing them, they need to be seen as kids. Maybe they can be reached. Maybe, all that's needed is the right approach. This is usually beyond the pale of schools. But governments can begin training specialists whose job is to reach out to gang leaders and work at healing them. Is that always possible? Maybe not even the majority of the time, but each time a leader is rehabilitated that's a pretty substantial outcome.

Bullying gets lots of attention because it's safe to focus on. It gives us clear perpetrators and clear victims. There are no competing philosophies involved, no sensitivities, no covering our own proclivities or secrets, no fear or ignorance in regard to intervention. We can use power to catch the culprit. Discipline. And bullying tragedies are sexy for the media. They get viewers or readers. It's comparable to the true crime story. Bad guys and good guys.

Schools develop anti-bullying strategies. Private businesses promote prevention manuals and training sessions. Teachers attend workshops. This all makes us feel good. It allows the school administration to publicize how proactive and on top of things it is. This may sound cynical, even though I do think schools do need to address bullying. What I object to is the jargon, the pat answers, and the reliance on paper descriptions that often don't go to the roots of the behaviour. Anti-bullying programs might help, but they may or may not be effective in any complete or lasting way.

If schools chose to ground themselves in the lived realities of the students, if they chose to respond to the lived needs of their students and built their curriculum and practices from that centre then bullying occurrences would be situational and short-lived. When schools are places of authenticity, teachers know the students, care about the students, engage in their reality and classes reflect that, then the dynamic that underlies bullying is treated.

Kids bully for two reasons - either they are hurt and want to displace that or they have modeled bullying and are acting it out. Their hurt has involved powerlessness, helplessness, victimization. I was asked to see a boy who had beaten up another boy. He didn't defend his actions. Instead he said, "I think I have a lot of anger. My dad works overseas for six months at a time, and I never get to see him." Case closed. Smart kid. Honest kid. He won't become a bully. His anger arises because he hurts. He longs for his father. That turns to anger because anger gives him power. He no longer has to feel sad. He no longer has to feel helpless. He can substitute his hurt for the adrenaline that comes with anger. That's better than hurt. It's better than loneliness. It's better than feeling powerless.

Bullying programs are often systemic or mechanical. A list of pointers. They don't address that boy's sadness over his missing dad. He needs help to cry. He needs ideas on how to communicate with his dad when he's away. The dad needs feedback about his absences. The family needs interaction to show them what's happening with their son. They need help to figure out some compensating practices. They might not be able to change the basic absence but they can improve on how it affects the boy.

This only happens when a school is based on relationships, in which adults are linked with the students in a caring and open way. When they know each other, then issues can be addressed.

There are times when relationships alone aren't enough. In their adolescent years there are too many factors all going on in teenagers development. No school can be on top of them all. So, there is a place for straight out discipline. The key in that regard is for every student in a school to be inculcated with a simple understanding - IT'S SMART TO TELL IF YOU'RE BEING HURT OR THREATENED. We need to ensure that every kid understands this to their core. The prevailing mindset is that telling an authority about a problem with another kid makes one a rat. Bullies like to use the rat term to mask their own culpability.

Victims of bullies are already taking a hit to their self-esteem so they don't want to add another one by seeing themselves as a rat. I keep a rubber rat on top of my computer in my office. He's a cute fellow and squeals when I squeeze him. I visit classrooms in elementary schools and in the lower grades of the high school to talk about sticking up for your rights. Primary are the right to say "OW!" and to tell the truth about your life. I try to help the kids understand that by keeping it secret when they are being threatened or hit, it means they are taking on the perpetrator's problem. The perpetrator needs to keep it secret because they are in the wrong. So, when the victim keeps quiet it supports the perpetrator's bad behaviour. I squeeze Mr. Rat and get them to laugh and see how misguided their assumptions are about opening up their plight.

I also address the potential bullies in the audience. I talk about how bullying comes from hurt and experience. How it uses anger or violence to lift their bleak sense of self, how it tries to override their own pain by inflicting it on someone else. Someone innocent. I explain how bullies will come up with excuses to justify why they need to hurt or threaten others, but that inside they know it's just because they want to do it, that it makes them feel good. They need to make themselves feel good in that way because they feel bad.

This gives everyone a chance to understand and in so doing weakens the readiness to secrecy. When kids fully understand something it leads to more confident and clear choices. By exposing the mechanics of bullying to them it also makes would-be bullies more self-conscious about carrying out their deeds. And, of course, I invite anyone in the class who is being bullied or is doing the bullying to come and see me afterwards so they can get their situations improved.

It is so important to see perpetrators as human, as coming from the same place as the victims. When we develop that kind of mindset then we are in position to change the whole dynamic. Kids don't want to be bad. They are inundated from the moment of birth with what being good looks like and with the rewards awaiting all of us when we are good - especially the social acceptance and approval, even accolades, from others. Kids want that. They want to be good. They feel guilty when they are bad. The number of "bad seeds" or truly deviant beings are infinitesimally rare. It is the kids who have been driven bad that we encounter.

When I get involved with kids who are bullying, I begin with the knowledge that they can be reached. I talk about their own experiences of being hurt. This is not to enter into therapy with them per se though that may eventually take place, but to establish an empathy for their victims. I want them to see themselves in their victim's place. I also want them to reflect on whether they want to see themselves as bad, as a bully. Teenagers, as a rule, don't conceptualize with any clarity how their actions portray them. Certainly no teenager I've ever met, if asked, would automatically state themselves to be a bully. Thus, I put it to them. This gives them a chance to do that reflecting, to decide if that's the role they want to be seen to have. Once having gotten them to remember times when they have been hurt I want them to decide if they want to be a hurter.

This works 90% of the time. Sometimes, the kid is so messed up, so wedded to that need for power, so unwilling to reflect, that I revert to the discipline default position. "If you insist on choosing to hurt, then the administration will suspend you or call the police or both."

One time, I learned a good lesson the hard way. Through patient counselling I'd gotten the aggressor to understand the error of her ways and when she left my office I reported that I thought the problem was solved and that the victim was now safe. A day later, the same victim was beaten up on the school bus by a couple of girls. My error? I had truth-fully gotten to the aggressor. She had meant what she said about a truce. But she hadn't told her friends about it. The friends took matters into their hands and attacked the unsuspecting girl. From then on I vowed to always say, "And you'll talk to your friends and ensure that they too lay off and not go after the other person right?"

The other part of the bullying equation, and the part too often ig-nored, is the make-up of the victim. Is there something going on within them that contributes to the dynamic? Some aspect of their behaviour or character that plays a role in the victimization?

PHILLIP - I was asked to start seeing Phillip when he was still in grade seven. His teachers were worried because he was often a victim of bul-lying. Of average size, Phillip had dark curly hair and wore glasses. We met three times altogether, and from our first meeting we had no trouble getting along. He was quite happy to have me as a contact for when he'd later go to the high school.

I learned that Phillip for some years had been a not infrequent target for other kids. His parents knew of it and were cynical about the school's capacity to protect their son. Phillip shared that cynicism. It became quickly apparent that he would be a tough kid to help. He had a resistance to altering his self-perception. He was convinced he had no power. No matter how I framed things, no matter what I suggested, he was absolute that it wouldn't work, nothing would change. He'd either already tried it to no avail or was just sure it wouldn't help. Instead of finding this frustrating, since I knew that in fact some of the ideas I was positing actually would have an impact, I realized that I was dealing with an impasse. Phillip had become wedded to his role. He saw himself as a victim, and his parents validated that. It was painful, but it was him and he had grown to accept it.

In some odd ways it gave his daily life a texture. He was a part of the peer scheme. He had attention, albeit negative, but still it was a place.

This is much the same as the kid who acts out disruptively in class. They get in lots of trouble, but they get attention and the negative attention is better than none at all. Plus they are in control of getting it so that gives them some sense of power, of ownership. Similarly with Phillip. He was somebody; he was the boy who got picked on.

I stopped seeing him after three visits because by then I had enough rapport that he would come to me in the following years if the need ever became paramount, and I knew that continuing counselling was not going to get anywhere. He had heard some new approaches. He could try them out if he wanted. If he didn't then he'd keep managing as best he could. He was familiar with the variables. I knew that in time he and his peers would move past the bullying stage.

Bullying can be divided into two categories - situational incidents and chronic patterns. The former are the instances when a tougher kid picks on a weaker kid because of something that happened. They are relatively easy to resolve. The dominant kid needs interception and needs to cease his intention to hurt, or, if the deed has already been done, he needs to apologize and understand what made him do it. Usually it's all about helping the aggressor see himself in the victim's shoes and see that there were other ways to handle it other than meanness. The victim needs to hear an apology and then let it go.

The chronic patterns can be more problematic. The one doing the bullying needs a counter relationship. They need a healthy and nourishing replacement for the scape-goating pattern they are engaging in. A bully needs the power, the rush, and the distraction that they get from the bullying activity. As mentioned before, another factor might be that the bully is experiencing similar behaviour at home. Maybe their dad is aggressive or overpowering towards their mom, maybe the dad or mom does that to them, and maybe an older sibling or stepsibling is doing that to them. All that negative input needs a release somehow. So, it's logical to in turn act out what one lives or what one models.

So, the needs of the bully are legitimate. Authorities ought not to just focus on eradicating the behaviour. It's not mechanical. Kids are not simply bad apples. The bullying behaviour is coming from someplace and it makes sense for the person to engage in it. Crap is being piled into them and they are trying to pile it out onto someone else. "Here victim, you take it."

Fundamentally, bullies must be understood as children, as evolving beings doing their best to survive and develop. They need our correction and guidance; they need our understanding and assistance to function with their own pain. When we do that, we reclaim a potentially lost child and avert future anti-social behaviour. We should be excited and pleased at such an opportunity. Nothing helps more than linking the child - whether 13 years old or 18 years old - with a genuinely caring adult who wants to have the link. This is a powerful step in countering the effects of whatever drives the bully.

We all want to be liked. We all value those positive, caring relationships in which we feel that our real selves are known by the other person and that we are liked because of who we are. So, when an adult takes the time to know the bully, to get the bully to lay out all the stuff going on in their life and still the adult likes the bully, then the medicine starts to work. Anger, loneliness, aloneness, and the feeling of being trapped are all lessened. The pressure abates. The bully starts to live again and to act rather than react or act out. The bully needs to tell their story fully.

Obviously, in the best-case scenario, the parents would be reached and be a part of the transformation. Their behaviour or unawareness would be addressed and they would make changes. Too often we don't have the skills or capacity to do this. Too often the parents are too much of the problem and are unwilling to seek help in changing their ways.

Nothing draws media attention quicker than tragedy or scandal. Any suicide of a teenager as a result of persistent bullying is a case in point for both, though it's unlikely that most recognize the scandal aspect. Each time one of these sad stories hit the airwaves, everyone seems to take notice. For a while. That's the point: it will have been far from the first person driven to suicide because of bullying. That's the scandal. We all know about the deep damage which bullying causes. The latest tragedy has only brought it to headlines once again.

And once again, there will be news commentary, quotes from experts and educators, tearful pleas from parents or others bereaved, and asserted commitment from school districts to enact anti-bullying programs. All talk. All forgotten about as soon as our attention is drawn elsewhere. That's both the tragedy and the scandal.

There are glossy brochures in every school in Canada which tout all manner of anti-bullying DVD's, manuals, and curriculum units that can be purchased "at special discount rates if acted upon now". Speakers are available to "train" teachers in how to make their schools bully-free zones.

But next year, there will inevitably be another similar death. And in the meantime, there will be thousands of kids of all ages living with unarticulated suffering because they are being bullied.

If we really wanted to, we could eliminate bullying in our schools and massively counteract its occurrence outside schools. All educational leaders have to do is to place it on the same level that they place curriculum. Most schools have there mission statement and a list of school goals adorning their front foyer - the code they supposedly consider as their governing direction. Just words. In practice, on a daily basis, schools are about the subjects being taught. That's where the energy goes and that's how they are evaluated. Death and suicide don't dent that ruling ethos.

We could change this. All we need to do is make it a priority to teach kids how to get along and respect each other. The curriculum needs to fit into that on a practical and observable basis. Values need to be taught. Communication needs to be taught. Every year. Self-awareness, resourcefulness, creativity, and self-care needs to be taught. Rights need to be taught. From the beginning to graduation.

I asked a grade 12 non-academic English class what they would do if any of them were the principal of a school in which a student committed suicide due to bullying. A 17 year old boy blurted out, "Close the school!" What he meant was he'd do something drastic because he would see it as needing drastic action that had to be responded to. In other words not just more words. A response that meant something, that sent a message.

More specifically, schools need to attack the underlying paradigm that countenances bullying. By definition we see bullies as stronger than victims. A person who allows him/herself to be pushed around or who doesn't fight back is a "pussy". When someone threatens you, the desired response is to "stand up" to the threat. Don't let them push you around. Thus, we establish within our kids a sense of failure just waiting to arise. We create a polarity of either or. You are a winner or a loser. A "man" or a "pussy". Fight back or run away. There are only two choices. To be afraid is bad.

Instead of giving the superiority to bullies, we need to teach kids about bullies, to expose the weakness of that behaviour, to advertise the weakness of that behaviour. Instead of posters that bleat about saying no to bullying, about standing up to bullying, we need posters that describe and explain how bullies get made, what goes on inside someone when they are bullying. Posters that say, "OF COURSE I"M AFRAID. WHO WOULDN'T BE AFRAID OF SOMEONE WHO HAS BEEN HURT AND NOW WANTS TO HURT."

We need to engage our students from the beginning in understanding what we are as humans. And we need to teach and elicit from them doable strategies to use when feeling any kind of threat. A sort of self-defense for the mind. When someone walks up and taunts, "I'm gonna kick your ass!" We need to have kids trained in a variety of responses, one of which is "What's wrong with you?"

A client of mine recently was assailed via email by racist threats made to her by someone she thought was a friend. She was hurt and scared. Despite her maturity and intellect, she did what most of us do, she accepted the other person's dominance and internalized the negativity - she felt bad. The other person did bad, but she felt bad.

By a stroke of ingenuity, she decided not to carry the hurt. Instead, she posted the racist attack on her own Facebook page and invited comment. By doing this, she instantly depersonalized the situation. She made the attack objective. Others then weighed in and condemned the vicious email. By taking charge of the situation instead of fighting back or absorbing the punishment, she transformed how she was affected. By taking charge and simply exposing the situation without her own commentary, she felt powerful. The burden was lifted. She was no longer a victim.

We naturally assume that we can teach kids how to do physics or carpentry or play an instrument. For some reason we don't want to teach them how to think and how to live.

BRYN – two brothers moved to our school from another province. Their reception was a bit strained. Both senior students, younger brother Shamus had an easier time than Bryn. Shamus was confident and personable, Bryn, not so much. Bryn also had always taken on the role as the protector of his younger brother. One day, another student was pushing around Shamus. Bryn stepped in a punched that kid in the face. A teacher quickly intervened, and Bryn was sent to the office. He was suspended for a week.

I was directed to initiate a five session program of anger management with Bryn. For some reason, we quickly developed a camaraderie and level of trust. My guess was that Bryn simply needed a place to feel relaxed and accepted. He had always had a quick fuse, knew how to fight, and, from past experience, had learned that the best defense was a good offense. The administration liked his brother Shamus, but viewed Bryn as a troublemaker, and they were looking for another incident to happen so they could rid him from the school for good. After just a few sessions, I discovered that inside, Bryn was actually a softie. He craved warmth and acceptance from a father figure. His dad had never been emotionally close and, in addition, was often drawn away from home for long periods because of his occupation.

One day about a month after Bryn had been re-admitted to school, I was told by another student that there was going to be a fight. The boy that Bryn had punched had assembled a couple of buddies, and there was a plan to surprise Bryn and thrash him. I was also told that Bryn knew of the plan and had begun carrying a knife to school. Obviously, if it was all true, this had become a deadly serious crisis.

I brought in Bryn for a talk. I confronted him about the knife. He immediately told me it was true, and that he was ready to use it if attacked. "If, I'm not prepared, they'll get me, and then I'll always be a target. It's not my fault. If they hadn't pushed Shamus, this would never have happened"

Then we talked. I explained how he could not win. Having a knife would label him in everyone's eyes as a troubled, hardcase. If he used it, he'd end up incarcerated. His future was at stake. There needed to be an alternative, and he needed to figure it out. I said I would stand by him.

We continued the conversation until it was decided that I should approach the other ones who were after him and try to reason them out of it. If that didn't work to my satisfaction, then we'd escalate it to bring in an administrator to forcibly defuse it. Bryn agreed. As he was getting up to leave, he reached into his pocket and pulled out a buck knife. "Here, you better keep this. I wasn't really comfortable with it, and if I don't have it on me, then I can't make a mistake."

As luck had it, the other boys accepted the mediation, and there never was an altercation. Given a bit of intervention, they all used it to their best interests. Bryn never did ask me for his knife back. I still have it.

Mean thoughts cloud my judgement
The fast and powerful fist makes faces bleed
More people come to see the circus
As the show ends
One person leaves the other with fresh blood

Simone Paul – 14 years old

11. Does Death Really Happen?

Probably the scariest initiative I've taken as a counsellor was setting up a death group. Unlike in India and other developing countries where death is a frequent and visible reality, our world in the West tends to maintain shelter from that. Especially when it comes to our children, we try to keep them from the upset surrounding death. Within families, it's probably talked less about than sex which is really saying something. So when it enters our lives and our children's lives, it tends to hit like a ton of bricks.

Grief is also something quite alien for most of us. Not the experience of it, which is inevitable, but the understanding of it, the preparation for it. Like so much else in our lives we think we can own it, control it. As though life needn't involve such helplessness, such a long-lasting process independent of us. Hence we also avoid grief.

There was a tragic death of a father in our community. A colleague phoned to suggest I go to the funeral and make overtures to the mother and mention to her that I was available for her two sons. One was a 10 year old and the other a 14 year old. The funeral service was emotional and filled with warm support from many. I took my place in the receiving line to give my condolences and to speak with the mother. She thanked me for coming and when I offered to be of support to her boys she again thanked me. Then she said, "They're actually handling it really well. I think they'll be fine."

Handling it really well. I wondered what that meant, and how that could be possible. In this situation I knew exactly what she meant. She meant that the boys were toughing it out. They hadn't fallen apart. They were holding it together, taking it. I could see the strain in their faces. The youngest was blank. The older boy was smiling tightly as he took people's hugs and hand shakes. No emotion.

Handling it meant no feelings and certainly no tears. Falling apart was bad. Showing the intensity of the deep pain and bewilderment from an unspeakable loss was a sign of failure. Taking it. Soldiering on. Going forward. Father dies five days before from an accident, but suck it up. Father who had been a pillar in their lives, was their existence, and suddenly was gone. The first awful introduction to **never** - as in never be with them again, and **forever** - as in gone forever. But don't fall apart.

I knew those kids were in for rougher times to come. Their loss and pain would be compounded by suppressed emotion, by cutting off from themselves, from their own hearts in order to escape facing the pain full on. And, unconsciously perhaps, to meet their mother's needs. To be "strong" for her. Be the way she wanted them to be.

There is no truth in any of this coping style. Because there is no truth there is no true strength. A loss of such a magnitude means we ought to fall apart. It means we ought to weep uncontrollably for days. That weeks and months later we should still be in deep sadness. I remember being in a town in Nepal and out of nowhere came three women all wailing and staggering from a lane. Two seemed to be supporting a middle one who was in the deepest distress. They were carrying on with much fanfare and open disarray. I later learned that the husband of the middle woman had died. They had begun their traditional grieving. Nothing was being hidden. On the contrary it was being brought out to the streets, to the public. I was told how there were well established steps for the grief to show itself throughout the following months and year. I have encountered similar traditional practices among the Sioux tribe, not as overtly emotional but filled with release and direct acknowledgement of the loss.

A genuinely strong person is one who faces their truth. We need to guide our children to this. Emotion is not weakness. When one has pain, one ought to be with that pain, feeling it, releasing the accompanying emotions for as long as those emotions are there. Often people ask me how long it takes to grieve a loss, how long the pain lasts. I reply that when someone breaks a leg that it heals when it does. Healing has no time schedule. And to say one heals from losing a parent or a child is perhaps misusing the term. Closer to accuracy is that the pain eases. The reality of the now will eventually allow the excruciating pain to become just an ache.

So it is far wiser to support and encourage a child to feel their sorrow. To release the energy and whatever words or sounds or actions that need to come out. I use art and artifacts to aid children with loss. That's if and when they come to me. The norm is for the kids to avoid counsellors when there is a great loss, so strong is the urge to hold it in. Holding it in means being able to function more easily. Priority is given to functioning, fitting in, doing, getting on with it rather than being with the truth of self. There is a penalty for this. It seems to work on the surface. You will see bereaved kids laughing and playing about, asking questions in class a couple of weeks after a death, and you would never think there had been any problem. But underneath they have walled a part of themselves away. When we do that, by definition we don't have all of ourselves. We don't have access to our full capacities. We don't feel the extent of the hurt, but then we don't feel the fullness of life around us, of our own life force. We are not whole. And it is likely that the internalized pain and the energy that goes to keeping it locked away will emerge in detrimental ways in the future.

Depression, physical ailments, phobias, less coping ability for stress - all of these can arise in later years from unresolved grief. None of this is profound or unknown. It's obvious. Yet adults abet their children in repressing. They allow the child to play the role of strength or to react as though "it's their way of coping, and everyone has their own way of coping." Bad coping is bad coping. Parents need to go with their kids when the bereavement occurs. Go with them into the grief. Go together or model the helplessness and the outpouring of deep sorrow. Seek help. Make it happen.

Insist on it. This doesn't mean immediately. It doesn't mean anything has to happen on any schedule. Parents should play it by ear. Watch. The kids need to catch their breath, need to digest what's exactly happened. Don't force something. Push. Join with. Ensure the feelings are coming out. Tears are strength. Tears set us free. They give us ourselves. They honor the dead. They strengthen the memories. Do what has to be done to make them happen. Especially with boys. Boys are so bludgeoned from their emotions, from showing their emotions, from acknowledging to themselves their own vulnerability that they need special assistance and support.

There is a touching and telling scene in an old popular movie called THE KARATE KID. The sensei, an old man named Myagi, has these superlative karate skills. He's a real master. Wise. He takes on the boy, the protagonist, as a student to teach him to protect himself from his peer bullies. The boy looks up to Myagi. The training is going well. Then one night the boy comes unexpectedly to Myagi's home. He spies on the old man who is in a small room that he's made into a shrine. In the shrine he has a picture of his wife who has died years before. Myagi is drunk and toasting her, talking to her, and intermittently crying. The karate master, a sage in full control of his emotions and reason knows to keep a door open to his heart through which he periodically allows the truth of his pain to flow.

ENRIQUE - Every year, schools have assemblies in which a speaker comes in to address drunk driving risks. Sometimes the speaker brings a visual presentation. Sometimes it's someone who has been a drunk driver with terrible consequences or someone who's been a victim of a drunk driver or lost a loved one. In one such assembly, paramedics had been presenting. They had described their jobs and the statistics, and the various penalties. Then they got into the visuals. They started showing slides of a crash site. Body bags appeared on the huge screen. All of a sudden there were the sounds of footsteps crashing down from one row to the next as someone was leaving the bleachers. It was all dark in the gymnasium. The slides kept changing and the paramedics continued talking. No one paid much attention as the crashing stopped, a door to the outside flung open and a boy left.

I realized right away who it was. I went around the other way to intercept the fellow. I found him outside the gym crying and hitting his head against the wall. It was Enrique. His father had been killed in a car accident two years before. Enrique could not stand seeing the images of the body bags. I put my arm on his shoulder and walked with him to my office. He sat down, put his face into his hands and wept. But not for long. The tears quickly turned to anger. He resented them showing the slides. In fact, he resented paramedics. In his mind he was convinced that his father could have been saved had the ambulance arrived sooner than it did. He wanted to speak about that. He wanted to be angry rather than hurt. And he also didn't want to stay with me very long. He agreed to come back later to talk.

Days later when he returned, he was chipper and smiling. He referred back to the assembly and said how it had caught him by surprise. He said he hadn't cried much before about his father's death. Enrique smiled all while he was telling me this. Then he said that he wasn't ready to face the fact that his dad had died. He did not want to go into those feelings. We talked about the advisability of going to that deep pain. He said he wasn't ready to because then his father would be dead. And he left. I never saw him about that issue again.

The reality was that Enrique did not want to go to that pain because he knew if he did that he would have to encounter the enormity of the truth, that his father was dead and gone, that he wasn't coming back, that he'd be alone without a dad forever, that his poor dad was really dead, had lost his life. It was too permanent. He couldn't go there. And by staying away from it he still had his dad. If he didn't face the truth emotionally, then his dad was not fully dead. This is a common impulse in all children, and probably an impulse we all share to a lesser degree. Don't want it to be true? Don't talk about it and it won't be. Don't think it and it won't be. Especially don't feel it.

Enrique never graduated. He left school early and found a job. I'd see him every so often and he'd always be smiling and friendly, ask of my well-being, give a laugh and then be off. As years went by, I learned he had linked up with a woman and her child. The child was twelve. I learned that Enrique drank too much and that he was an erratic and abusive, demanding stepparent. The youngster lived in misery. I guess Enrique wasn't prepared to give what he had, years before, lost the chance of ever having.

Death does put bystanders into a quandary. We don't know what to say. We don't want to intrude or bring a person down by mentioning or asking about the loss. We avoid the topic, act like it never happened. That makes us comfortable, and we believe makes it more comfortable for the bereaved. Keep it light. Of course no bereaved wants to talk about the loss over and over with everyone they know and meet. Especially kids don't want to come back to school and run the gamut of having every other kid come up to them and ask them how they are doing. They don't want the attention. They don't want to be singled out or under the spotlight. They want to be treated as they always were.

So it is hard to know what to say and do. Teachers and students usually feel uncertain and ask how to approach it. Though most teens are self-conscious and, if asked, would not want attention, I think it's a mistake to just go along with that impulse and validate the "secrecy" or "privacy". If every kid in school came up to the bereaved teen, put their hand on his shoulder or nodded, and said, "I'm sure sorry for your loss." or "I'm with you, _____.", it might be overwhelming but it would also send a message that the teen is cared about. And far fewer than every student would want to say anything, so the ones that do would be conveying that the bereaved person was not alone in their school community.

Specifically, I think if you've always been close or relatively friendly with the bereaved person then continue that by speaking of the death with as much length as you'd usually speak about any topic you shared. If you've been more of a distant friend, then just do the one-liner and keep it short and sweet, letting the bereaved know you care. For the five or so who are closer friends, hugs are appropriate. A quick hug when in public is such a statement of support and public valuing. Kids need that. Kids need to know they are valued, especially in their times of need.

Words I would avoid are "How are you doing?" They are such automatic greetings that they have lost any real meaning or intimacy. When used with a bereaved person they are burdensome and almost stupid. A friend of mine who lost his wife of decades said he wanted to get a t-shirt with the words printed on it, "DON'T ASK ME HOW I'M DOING". He was irritated and worn out by the never-ending query. "How do you think I'm doing? I'm doing shitty. I hate it. How do you think I'd be doing?"

It is more accurate and helpful, if you genuinely want to know, if you genuinely have the closeness to inquire, to use these words: "Hi, _____, so, what is it like today? Or "Do you feel like taking about your dad today?" The latter is pointed, but it's honest, and it gives the bereaved both respect and permission to say yes or no.

It is our awkwardness around death that led me to consider forming a support group of sorts for kids in our school who had lost a parent. I had been counselling a couple of different kids who had recently had a parent die. The sessions were rich and meaningful. I realized that I personally knew of fifteen others who had lost parents. I also knew that it was likely they had never been allowed or helped to grieve fully. And for sure I thought it would be very meaningful for them to be in the company of peers who had suffered in a similar way, who were dealing with a similar predicament.

I also knew that I was scared to actually gather these kids together. None of them were thinking about it, let alone requesting it. I knew it was going outside the lines that had naturally formed, that is, keeping private, not talking, and not sharing deep feelings. As well, I wasn't sure how to conduct the meetings. There needed to be some structure but to follow a mechanical group discussion format or with me putting the participants into roles or overly steering the proceedings would be an immediate turn-off. Teenagers aren't eager to be part of some "counselly" thing. They don't see themselves as "needing help".

To start with I asked the two who I was seeing if they thought it was a good idea for bereaved kids to know each other and get together to share experiences. They had questions. Among them were the concerns that it had to be voluntary, had to be private, and had to not follow a specific agenda. Let it flow.

My next challenge was how to call a kid in and say, "Hi there, I know your dad died three years ago and I wonder if you'd like to be in a group to talk about it?" For those I knew and had spoken with it would be easier but still clumsy and intrusive. For those I didn't know it would be like a bomb blast. Kids are going about their day in school absorbed by all the demands and stresses that come with a teen's life and out of the blue, some counsellor yanks them into his office and wants to get them to talk about their dead mom! How asinine is that?

For the only time in my career, I was scared to talk to kids. Nothing gave me an in. They had not done something needing my involvement. They had not asked for my involvement. There was no admistriviality for me to lean on. Just my knowledge - which they mightn't have given out - that one of their parents had died. There was no way around it. If I was going to try to start a group and there turned out to be one then I couldn't not be inclusive, I couldn't not at least invite those who qualified, at least give them an option.

It was all fumbly. No way around the clumsiness. I called the kids in one at a time over a period of a week. I started by saying that I had been working with a couple of kids independently of each other who had lost a parent and that in the course of our conversations it became clear that it would be really helpful if they could hear each other. I broached them about getting together and then realized there were others in the school who might be interested.

Each person I asked had immediate questions. When? Who? How many? What would they have to say? Did they have to go or stay if they didn't like it? Was this some kind of group counselling thing? Who's going to know about it? Some kids were eager and even asked if I had already asked so and so. Some said they'd give it a try. Three said not interested.

I arranged with their teachers to allow them out of classes for an hour during last class on an agreed upon afternoon. Also, as agreed upon, I didn't tell their teachers what they were leaving to do. I had us come to a vacant classroom to which I locked the door. In the room I had the desks in a circle and put soft drinks in the middle. If they want it everyone needs to have something to hold onto in trying times.

Eventually, all fourteen of the kids - from varying grades - arrived at the room. The nervousness was palpable. Silence. Waiting. What was this going to be? I breathed in. I was nervous, probably more than they were. Yikes. Now what. Open up the can of worms. Access emotions and thoughts that had been put away months and years before.

For what? Because some stupid counsellor thought it would be a good idea? I breathed in.

And we started. I reaffirmed that the meeting was voluntary, that it was confidential, that they didn't have to speak any more than they wanted to, that when they left the room that no one should try to continue on any of the discussion that had occurred unless the other person was fully willing, that no one else knew that they were in here or why they had left their normal class for the hour. I explained how we would take turns and that when someone spoke no one should try to tell them how to think, give advice, or comment in any way other than to acknowledge how it had affected them and then to speak about their own issue. This rule had been successful in my peer counsellor trainings, so I knew it would provide some emotional safety in this group too. Finally, I said that they all belonged to a unique club. That no one else in the school could know what it was like to belong in this group, but when they now looked around into each others' faces they could know that each one there could actually understand.

Then I asked each to take turns and introduce themselves and the parent who had died, and when and how. That done, some of the tension dissipated. Each of them now had a bit of a context for everyone else. They had heard other voices and heard their own voice being listened to. They had gone in the circle and seen how the format played out.

Next I asked them to continue going in turns but this time to focus more on what the death was like for them when it occurred, what some of the events were like around the death, what did they feel at that time. If they did not want to talk I said they could just say pass. But each kid talked when it was their turn. Some shook. Some cried. But each kid talked. This proved far more emotional, and it was clear that none of them had finished expressing what had been inside, some of them for a number of years.

As the session ended, one student asked if we were going to meet again. All agreed they wanted more. So, we set another meeting for two weeks time. When that session came, I suggested that each talk about how they thought they had been affected by having a parent die. Again it was emotional. Following that meeting, we met three more times and then brought it all to a close.

What had happened was that kids unconnected to each other had gotten a chance to feel less alone, less singled out by fate. They had been able to hear for the first time how others had gone through similar emotions to them. Instead of the cloister of the family within which to measure and experience their grief and loss and the accompanying limitations due to relationships or needs of others, they were finally free to be, to experience just their own feelings. This is such a beneficial process because aside from the release and catharsis and healing that can occur it also marks a step in their own individuation.

One girl said that after the first meeting she had driven to the spot where her father's truck had gone off the road and crashed. She had never gone there before, but she wanted to then. At the second meeting she told of how that affected her, how she had cried but felt afterwards that something had been completed inside her that she had been holding off. None of this had been conscious to her before.

ALICE - Another girl, Alice, had only tentatively agreed to attend the first meeting, stating she didn't think she "needed it". This, by the way, is an immediate response from most kids who have suffered a death in the family - they resist talking about the loss and opening up to it because they say they don't need to. Alice, a grade twelve student, had lost her father to suicide three years before. For the rest of the school year after the suicide I knew she had spent a lot of time doing her schoolwork outside the classroom. She was receiving regular grief counselling from an outside counsellor and her family was very active in attending to her needs and those of her younger brother. I had asked her if she was interested in the group meetings with a sense that she was one person who actually might not need them.

At the first meeting, Alice came in more relaxed than anyone else. She was checking it out. As people took their turns, she listened intently. When it was her turn, she spoke at length and in detail about the day of her father's death and the interactions that led up to him shooting himself with a rifle. Her younger brother, a grade nine, was also in the group. Other than him none of the rest was dealing with a suicide. Everyone's eyes were wide as Alice spoke. None were so intimately involved in the actual death of their parent. Alice broke down and cried several times as she spoke. But it did not deter her from continuing. She concluded by saying that this whole experience had totally surprised her, that she had believed she had worked all of her grief through, but that she felt really glad she had come and looked forward to the next meeting. Needless to say, this kind of modeling is worth it's weight in gold.

TYRELL - When her brother's turn came, he also spoke and cried. His situation was slightly different from his sister's and he spoke about that a bit. He was outside when his father killed himself and, unlike her, did not know what was unfolding upstairs. Whereas Alice had been thrust into the actual life and death drama and received the expected counselling reactions, Tyrell was on the periphery. He was an elementary school student when the event had occurred and his counselling had not been as intense and had not gone to the core of his loss and the emptiness from discovering rather than witnessing the suicide. Plus, he was a boy, and he had lost his same sex parent. The figure he had grown to see himself as had chosen to leave them all, had not valued his son enough to stay. The tangles within Tyrell's grief had not been engaged.

Because Alice had so graphically opened the door, modeled emotional permission to speak and feel, she had also nullified any shame that Tyrell might have felt. Her courage had reduced any fear or reticence Tyrell had about facing the group and telling everyone that, unlike them, his dad had killed his own self. So, Tyrell opened up and cried. This was particularly important because, while everyone in the school knew about the suicide, no one, obviously, spoke out loud about it around Tyrell, or he around them. It was like it had never happened. By being able to open up and describe it while facing his peers, it allowed Tyrell to be himself, to affirm his equality and his identity amongst his peers. To talk about what was never talked about, and in so doing activate the truth that though it was about his life, it was not him. It was his father.

This is powerful stuff and so difficult to get to with one on one counselling alone. A counsellor is an adult. Kids need to figure their issues out, integrate them and lay them to rest in the context of their own reality which, as teens, means in terms of the teen/peer milieu that is so acutely their world. Teens are in the stage where they hyper view themselves in comparison to the group - how do they measure up, how do they look, are they liked, are they good enough, normal enough. So when there is a deep secret or a pivotal aspect that has to be held apart it works against both peace of mind and sense of worth. It splits the being. When teens can hear the truth about each other and all the accompanying fears and doubts and frailties, they can accurately assess that indeed they fit, they belong, they are as good as anyone else. They can experience that through their own direct evaluation rather than being told it by an adult who in their mind might either not really know or who is just trying to make them feel good.

Tyrell and I had a counselling relationship before the group. I knew he had lots of work to do to integrate his pain and loss. He would invariably come into my office with a smile on his face. We'd chat a bit about how things were going and he'd insist that all was well. Then after a few minutes he'd start to tear up, and, by golly, there would be his dad again and all the residue of that terrible reality. For Tyrell, it was so necessary to have access to someone who would walk with him into the horror. Like post traumatic stress disorder (which in essence is what comes from suicides, sexual abuse, and all manner of childhood explosions), the key to healing is spitting out all the details and held-on-to feelings and conclusions, spitting them all out from the inner depths where they reside, until there really is nothing much to spit out anymore.

Tyrell needed to make sense of it all, in all its ramifications. Why did his dad do it? What did it say about his value to his dad? Would depression be a factor in Tyrell's life as he aged? What could have been done to stop it? Could something happen to my mom? Why me? Lots of talking, lots of sorting, lots of connecting, and lots of crying. Tyrell was up for it. Luckily for both he and Alice, their mother was or had been forced to become a strong and honest woman. She walked into the horror and supported her kids doing the same. She was part of their solution by how she took care of herself and sought her own help.

Tyrell looked up to his older sister. She chose to open up in the meeting. She cried. He, thus, had all the reinforcement he needed to walk the same route. Together they were a powerful gift to the others in the group. And to me.

Courage inspires courage. Truthfulness and transparency inspires truthfulness and transparency. Opening up to oneself inspires someone else to do the same. Throughout his manhood, Tyrell will continue to need to stay open to the residue and effects of his father's suicide. Those are all deeply etched into his psyche. While it is true that some aspects, perhaps even the most effecting ones, can be released and integrated if full treatment occurs at the time of the incident, there are other ramifications which only show themselves as time passes and life stages emerge. Thus, we may think we have "dealt with" or "healed" from a trauma, yet find ourselves living out a part of it many years later - despite the good work we did when we were younger.

The teenagers that I have worked with have taught me to continually look at my own behaviour and moods and life as a process. This means looking for and opening up to my own traumas and truths and how they have been etched into my psyche. How they seep out years later after I thought I had healed or resolved them. Like time-lapse vitamins our traumas and childhood experiences emerge in ways we would not anticipate or spot. Tyrell is well on his way to becoming a happy and successful man, but he has not healed. None of us have. We are, if we choose to be, in the process of healing. Of becoming the selves we were born to be rather than the results of events or circumstances around us as we grew up.

When I was little my mom died

Crispy wind
bites your fingers as you
grab some snow
you throw it
as it gains speed
heading at your brother
you duck behind the van
the van that has carried
everything
the past
the future
and the present
great memories
of birthdays
and sad ones
of going to the
airport with your mom
you grin as you look
back at your brother
and throw
another one

Vanessa Morrison – 14 years old

12. Suicides

There have been a number of kids who have committed suicide during my years as a counsellor. With each case, I recognized that I had failed whether I directly knew the teen or not. This isn't a case of personalizing or guilt or aggrandizing my own position. It's simply being accurate. A school counsellor ought not be a reactor. Ought not to be someone who sits back and waits for kids who have needs to come forward. An effective counsellor is someone who is proactive, who's formulating methods and programs that reach out to the student body. A flat poster announcing that a troubled teen should phone such and such a telephone line or make an appointment to see a counsellor just doesn't cut it.

In this era of speed and busyness in which daily life is cluttered in unprecedented ways, students in schools need some counter force at play. They need an intrusion of "Hello, let's slow it down a bit and just pause for a moment; this is who we really are. ...." This is done by holding assemblies, regularly visiting classes, bringing in speakers, and presenting vivid and compelling video presentations in which serious subjects are broached.

To look at a school from the outside, one sees a happy, busy community all intent on classroom subjects, sports and fine arts. Social events like dances, spirit days, and visiting entertainment groups augment the milieu. All nice and easy. That the vast majority of the kids live with serious challenges - a drinking parent, a drugging parent, poverty, abuse, mental health issues in the home, a single parent, workaholic parents, blended families, fighting parents, distant parents, or unhappy parents to name a few - does not enter into the reality of the school. This is comparable to the traditional approach to an alcoholic - don't talk about it, act like it isn't there.

To be fair, some argue that a school needs to be a respite from chaos and uncertainty. That's certainly true. But being a respite doesn't have to mean operating in a totally separate dimension. More likely, schools don't structure in the real life issues because they fear to and don't know how to. Delivering curriculum is easy. It's mechanical and safe. Opening up to the underlying chaos or pain in our lives might mean losing control. So schools pretend. School life is a pretend life.

I remember being in front of a grade assembly in the gymnasium. I was one speaker of several. Others were conveying various information - a school dance, study habits, club information etc. Then it was my turn. I got up and started talking about how so many live with alcoholic parents or with abuse in their lives. Man, you should have seen that assembly come alive. They couldn't see each other because they were all sitting in bleachers facing me. I could see all of them. What had been a relatively still, patient group of two hundred suddenly became a fidgeting mass. There was no talking just body movements. A nerve had been hit.

Thus it is the counsellor's responsibility to ensure that every teen has learned how common the underlying traumas in life are, and **are given evidence that they can be addressed**. Too often there is too much emphasis on describing the issue such as child abuse or drug abuse and not equal attention to the actual route out of it. Any presentation on a serious personal subject needs to finish with a confident and precise explanation of what a teen can do if they face such a situation and why it will help make their lives better.

None of us particularly advertise our shames or the difficulties we face. We keep them inside. This isolates us as well as insulates us. It leads us to take on the belief that no one else has the same problem even if common sense says that can't be the case. It leads us to believe the difficulty has more power than it has. Holding it in secret also prolongs the situation. If it isn't talked about, if it isn't alleviated or resolved than the repercussions last that much longer, the shame and habits that emerge from it become a more entrenched part of our life. So a counsellor wades into the fray and initiates examination and discussion of life difficulties. The counsellor makes sure that the students know there are attainable and facile steps that can be taken to remedy the situation. The emphasis must be that, while some things can't be outright erased or fixed, they can all be improved. The counsellor needs to mention what can be done and how it works to improve conditions and lessen the weight.

The teenage years are one of the highest risk stages for suicide. We all know this. As mentioned before in this book, teenagers are in the precarious position of being at the end of naivete. They recognize and compute the dysfunctions in their lives/families yet they still feel powerless to change them. Their emotional cores are in great flux. These emotions peak and fall at unpredictable times. They feel so deeply and acutely more than ever before in their years of existence. What to do about dilemmas? What to do about shame? What to do about overwhelming burdens? The consideration of dying to fix it all, logically pops into every teen's head.

Suicide prevention programs are always set up as one-shot affairs. When they happen, and that is infrequently, a speaker will meet with students, give them information, show a video, have them do some exercises and then leave. They never come back and there is no process to refresh, re-teach, or check on the well-being of the students. The one shot occurrence is considered sufficient - as though it was an inoculation for tetanus. In some schools even this may never happen in a student's years there.

The problem is that students are growing and changing every few months. What they encountered or learned about in grade nine is forgotten by grade eleven. The good thing is that kids often look out for one another. The vast majority of suicide interventions that I've been involved with have come about through kids coming to me worried about someone they know. That's why the first line of defence against suicide must be activating that natural propensity in students to care about each other. Instead of focusing on the symptoms that one should be aware of in themselves, greater emphasis should be placed on urging kids to watch out for the symptoms in others. Each school should have a banner at the entrance and before the student body in each assembly - "BE THERE FOR EACH OTHER".

Because it's so normal for kids to be watching their peers anyway for style, behaviour, antics, whatever, it follows that they are the best ones to notice changes or symptoms that indicate someone is at risk. They just need cuing in that direction. They need to be assured that being a good friend, being a good human being means paying attention to the well-being of others and taking action to support that well-being. Kids are mortified at the thought of being a rat. They will keep secret all manner of atrocities to not be seen as a rat. But when it comes to suicide it is easy to trump that code. The simple appeal to friendship is all it takes.

On a practical level, kids value friendship above all else in their lives (families accepted). Suicide awareness presentations need to be explicit in the affirmation that true friendship means doing whatever is necessary to save someone's life. If there is a suspicion that someone may be suicidal, if they are showing symptoms of withdrawal, depression, self-anger, etc. then being a good friend means attending to those symptoms. It means bringing them up directly with the peer or going to a professional to bring them up. To do otherwise means to be prioritizing one's worry about one's own image or needs rather than the friend's life. When this is put directly to teens they get it.

So, I failed to prevent the suicides in my schools because I wasn't proactive enough. I didn't set up on-going interactions to educate and activate the student body with regard to suicidal symptoms. I did nothing to educate the students about depression, about how prevalent and untreated it is amongst teenagers. No counsellor or teacher can watch or know about every student in a school. But someone can watch or know about every student in a school. The students themselves can watch each other's backs. They just need the tools and direction to do that. My contribution to that was insufficient.

Depression and impulsivity, in my opinion, are the two key components in suicide attempts. Depression so weighs on the teen, so convincingly leads to hopelessness or despair, that without enough life experience to help them see how everything changes, how ups and downs are fluid and no down is permanent or as bad as it seems, death seems an answer. Just as the marketers and the proponents of rampant consumerism hold sway in Western society, so it follows that impulsiveness has been nurtured. Buy now, don't wait. Get it while it's hot. When it comes to anger and hurt, impulsivity makes a bad mix.

Anger at an unchanging parental situation or rage and pain at a relationship break-up, teens feel it so acutely. Death is dramatic. And it's easy. I have had teens in my office of both genders who were beside themselves with anguish at the sudden loss of a love relationship that was so serious, so definitive - one that had been going on for a long time, a full three months. In their own words they say, "I don't know what I will do. It's the end of the world."

This is why we worry so much about copycat scenarios when a suicide does occur. We realize we don't know the level of precariousness within each individual in the school, so we don't know what doors a suicide might spring open for others. Schools are wise to measure their responses to suicides. If they make too much of it, if the victim is celebrated too much then it does set a standard that others in their bleakness might see as attractive. It is common for people to imagine the fanfare that might result from their death and, as magical as it sounds, covet that attention.

We don't do any training on depression in schools and we don't do any training on relationships and what break-ups will entail emotionally. This is a part of the real world that doesn't exist in schools. Everyone learns on their own and the hard way. It should not be and need not be. It's almost unfathomable that mathematics equations are deemed more important!

DINAYA - It was after midnight and I was still up. I was just finishing the newspaper from the neighbouring town and had come to the classifieds section. That section begins with obituaries. My body lurched forward, and I could feel that terrible sensation of shock and fear rush out of my skin as I saw Dinaya's beautiful young face above her name and the worst words in the world, "We regret to announce..." It was a photo of her when she was two years younger, when I had been seeing her on a semi-regular basis until she had changed schools. Her dark, black curls framed a smile that beamed from the page.

Dinaya had died at 18 years of age. When she was 14 years old, her parents had split up. Unable to connect with her mother's new beau, she had remained with her father whom she loved dearly. Still, she was a girl without a mom. Dad could not replace that. Plus, dad worked a lot and had financial troubles. So Dinaya did what so many teens do, she turned to friends for emotional support. Those teens used drugs. Dinaya's extended family tried to help. An aunt brought her into her home in the town where my school was. That's how I became involved. Issues arose over curfews and school work undone and other frictions.

Her aunt was very supportive and well meaning, but there was really nothing that could give Dinaya what she wanted. There would be no family getting back together and no mother. Dinaya flirted with drugs. She struggled with depression but she managed. I had hopes for a bright future for her. Her smile and good humour were compelling. And she was honest with me. Her drug use, though not excessive, was still a concern for her. But it served a purpose. As months went by, Dinaya decided to move back to her father's house. I talked on the phone with her but did not see her again.

A year later, I got a phone call from the neighbouring province. Dinaya was working there and relatively happy. She was still dabbling occasionally with drugs and we talked about that. It was good to hear from her.

Then the obituary. I later learned that she had gotten into an unhealthy relationship with a drug user. My assumption is that Dinaya simply got caught between her own aware wisdom and her growing dependency on drugs and the unfortunate circumstances of finding a partner who would abet that dependency. She knew herself, knew her pain deeply, knew her life should be more but gave up on hope that it would become so. Dinaya did not yet realize how life moves, how the circumstances and feelings of youth shift. She saw her stage as forever, saw her pain as everlasting. She got lost in that and took her own life. I still grieve for her.

Dad:

Why don't you spend time with me when I'm at your house? It feels like every time I'm at the cabin you spend the whole time doing chores. If there arent jobs to do, you usually start building something. It hurts, and it almost feels like you're trying to avoid me. When we do spend time together, it is usually something like hiking. I don't like hiking, once in a while is fine but when we hike almost every weekend, it gets boring. It seems like to spend time with you I have to do a lot of things I don't like, and I don't think that's fair. Please stop trying to convince me I'm out-of-shape, I think I'm healthy enough, and I don't have any urge to get in better shape. Just because you and _____ like to get lots of strenuous exercise doesn't mean I do.

DEVI - 14 YEARS OLD

The lake all alone
dying in a field of mud
the sun shattering the moon
when I die the lake will be there
BLUE   GREEN

Jessica Fleury – 13 years old

About two years ago my grandma put me in a home. It was like jail they had plastic on the windows and bars over that. They had a big door in all the rooms that was magnetic. The door had a alarm that everyone would hear they gave me a room that had two beds in it.

And two big coberds that you whould have to put your stuff in one of them. They had this room me and my friends called it the death room. Because when you wheren't good they would grab you hard and throw you in there. If you fought they would beat you until you would stop horsing around. They sed they liked us but I know that they didn't. They had this step thing. If you were good they would put you up a level. If you where bad, bad I ment thoughtless, they would hit you and beat you and they whouldn't stop fore about one houre. Once they threw me in the death room and started herting me. I kicked on of the staff right in the grind. They left me in the bad room for one houre and I was sow mad. I started whacing my head against the wall and it started bleeding. Sow I stopped. Then I started punching the metal door and I brock my fist. Then they let me out because I hert myself. Once my friend was liping off and three staff members started herting him. They wouldn't tell are parents that they hert us they gust sed that we were out of controll. I don't whant to say anymore. Thanks for reading my real story.

GARTH – 14 years old

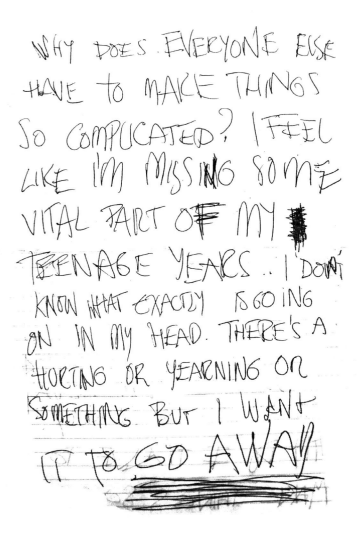

WHY DOES EVERYONE ELSE
HAVE TO MAKE THINGS
SO COMPLICATED? I FEEL
LIKE I'M MISSING SOME
VITAL PART OF MY
TEENAGE YEARS.. I DON'T
KNOW WHAT EXACTLY IS GOING
ON IN MY HEAD. THERE'S A
HURTING OR YEARNING OR
SOMETHING BUT I WANT
IT TO GO AWAY

Allen – 14 years old

Conclusion

I wonder how many of us have been driving along a road and come upon a group of teenagers walking in the same direction? Instead of snuggling over to the side as one might assume pedestrians would when a vehicle approaches, they keep walking well out in the lane, completely oblivious or non-caring about said vehicle coming up behind them. We honk, slow down, shake our heads at the indifference or arrogance we imagine going on inside their heads. Or a similar occurrence. At the beach, in a mall, out on the sidewalk .... teenagers in a group swearing away, loudly discussing any outrageous topic they are into, not a moment of concern for who might be in the vicinity. Grrrr! *What's this world coming to?,* we mutter. Of course, this latter scenario more and more often plays out at sporting events and the same beaches only the boorish behaviour comes from adults, especially younger male adults.

And there's some of the explanation. Kids model from their elders. When adults see nothing wrong with foul language, then why should kids show any discretion? Logically, the refrain is instantly on their lips - *it's only words; you swear all the time.*

When the teens are taken aside and engaged in an actual discussion of why they are using bad language or behaving obnoxiously in public, the rest of the explanation becomes clear. The crux of the matter is that they have not been sufficiently taught about respect, about others and how their behaviour or language might affect others. Of course, they've heard the words in elementary school and as young children. There are signs posted in secondary school hallways. But all of that is overridden by experience. These kids model coarseness and self-centredness all the time. And they are inundated with so many trillions of other words and messages that there is no way the ones about respect can have any meaning, and internalized reality.

We do not train kids in respect. We do not reward them for respect. We do not make the living of respect seem important. As parents, in our busyness, our compulsion to live life to the fullest, to get our kids into every activity we can find, we don't take the time to emphasize or engage our kids in the meaning of respect or why it is essential. Nor do our high schools go into it. Teachers bitch about lack of respect and they certainly want and expect it, but they don't do anything to promote the learning of it.

Before our school trips to India, I coach everyone over many sessions prior to the trip. Going away from home over Christmas is tough for most kids and going into the unpredictable cauldron of India magnifies it all a hundred times over. They needed to learn about the culture and history. They needed to learn about the numerous challenges that they would encounter - lack of sanitation and toilet facilities, squalor, noise, crowdedness, harassment, theft, illness, poverty, and sadness. I ran them through assertiveness exercises. But underlying everything we did in preparation, was the theme of respect and of staying open to learning, staying open to the raw humanity we were to enter.

No one can truly prepare to travel to a country like India. There is simply too much that is alien, too much that overwhelms, stimulates, and intrudes on one's being. It's all viscerally real, viscerally alive, and that's the point of taking kids there. It's not easy, and it's not fun.

KINESHA - One girl who came on the second trip was Kinesha. She was only 14. I'd usually not allow someone so young to go on such an arduous, emotionally demanding trip. But she was keen. I decided to let her go after I talked with her about her personal life. She immediately brought up serious challenges she had encountered in her younger years - separations from her mother, home violence, and loneliness. It was her willingness to share those deep sadnesses that convinced me she could handle India. She was not hiding the awful truths in her own life, so it was obvious she would embrace the awful truths that India might push at her.

Kinesha's family was far from wealthy. For over seven months she plugged away on her own at garage sales, bottle drives, babysitting, and eliciting sponsors. She raised her own money.

As with the first trip, this one exposed all of us to daily trials. Rather than minimize or rationalize away the children begging at our arms, the mothers with newborns, we asked the students to open up to that reality. Rather than find ways to dismiss it, we asked that they imagine what life would be like living that way, regardless of whether it came about because a "pimp" ran them, whether they secretly had enough to live on without begging, or whether giving would only encourage more begging. Regardless of any of the underpinnings which they could not be sure of, we asked them to imagine the life of the child doing it. We asked them to feel.

Our trip over three weeks makes its way across northern India on night trains. Towards the end, we spend two days volunteering in Mother Teresa's charities in Kolkata. The group is split into three sections and each goes to a different venue. Kinesha went to Shishu Bhavan, the home for abandoned children and babies, many physically or mentally handicapped. There among the tiny metal cribs, Kinesha went about ministering to the needs of children. One little girl with limbs so tiny in circumference that Kinesha's fingers more than circled them was her favorite. But another little boy, maybe two years old, has stayed more clearly in her mind. She wrote in her journal, "*One of the women who works there was busy attending to various chores. This little boy started calling for more food. I wanted to get him some but was told I couldn't. The worker came over to him and slapped him on his cheek. Not hard but hard enough. She looked at me and smiled as though to say, nothing was wrong, but the little boy was crying. I waited for her to go away and then I went over to sit beside the child. He kept crying. I put my arm around him and kissed him on the head. It was really sad. I could feel the scars on his head with my lips.*"

Later on, a couple of days later after we had gone to a beach town on the Bay of Bengal to decompress from the all the strenuousness and emotional endurance of the trip I heard this violent retching in the room next to mine. It had started at about 10:30 P.M. After another hour and about two more retchings, I decided to check on who was so sick. It was Kinesha. She came to her doorway. We sat down together on the marble floor. By then it was close to midnight. Everyone else was asleep.

We talked about how the trip had been for her. I gave her an anti-biotic pill and a bit of water to wash it down. Because she had thrown up so much, a few minutes later I gave her an anti-nausea pill to dissolve in her mouth in order to keep the anti-biotic down. Almost immediately she turned her head away from me and vomited. So much for the medications.

I helped her back to her bed. Her roommate was sound asleep. Just as we got to her bed, she stepped in some wetness on the floor and said, "Oh, I forgot, I threw up some there too." Then she got into bed and tried to sleep. She vomited a couple more times that night. The next day she still felt nauseous and ate only a couple of bananas. Most of the group went on a great day trip to an inland salt lake for a village tour and a swim on a deserted beach. Kinesha stayed behind, too sick to move around. When all the rest returned that evening they were in high spirits. They had even seen dolphins. Kinesha just shrugged her shoulders. She didn't need more. For her, the trip was complete, and she had already embraced the fullness. The sickness was simply her turn at that and nothing more.

Another event on this same India trip emphasized who teenagers are, who they can be. On Christmas Day, we were in Varanasi, the holiest city of Hinduism. It is a city of mesmerizing activity, clamor, and substance - a vortex of living and dying. We were staying in a guesthouse right by the Ganges River. Everyone the day before had bought presents for under $5 for a secret Santa gift exchange.

We gathered together in a rough circle with all the creatively wrapped gifts in the middle. Despite being away from home and family, energy was high and joyous. One by one the gifts were given out and opened by the recipient. Colourful silk scarves, carvings, woven bags, fragrant oils - lots of neat stuff. Then mine came. It was a string tied roll of two small pages of paper with a single green pea pod in the middle. "You have to read it out," said Sylvannah, a slight 17 year old who I had observed to be somewhat timid, maybe struggling with the trip to that point. And so I unrolled the pages and read:

> *"In India there are so many things you can do with 200 rupees, especially if you know how to barter. With so many options how could I possibly know what choice would be something you would remember even just one year from now. It's easy enough to buy you some gift you would appreciate for a while. For some reason I felt I needed to give you more than the material. So, I bought 22 oranges, 7 carrots, a big bag of snap peas, and two tomatoes. I gave them out on the streets. It was so gratifying, for both the giver and receiver, to give to those who weren't asking, but have need. These people don't have the means to purge themselves in celebration and festivities like we do, especially at home.*
>
> *Oftentimes I hear the ramblings at home about the "spirit of Christmas". Today that concept was real to me. Out there in the middle of one of the most panicked streets I have ever stood in my life, full of people - who for the most part - will not be doing a single thing to celebrate Christmas, I experienced the most precious and true moment of Christmas I can recall. I cannot think of a single thing I could give you in the markets that are of any comparison to the fact that hungry*

*stomachs were filled, crushed spirits were given an unexpected hope,
and sad faces a smile.*

*Honestly, I didn't go out and change the world today. I did - through
me you did - however, make a difference, how much we'll never know.*

Merry Christmas!
Sylvanah"

She did this after being in India for only eight days. She had to leave
the ease of the area right around our guesthouse in Varanasi and go out
into the mayhem and cacophony of a truly helter skelter street area and
then have the gumption to buy food and approach people to give it away.
This was a big thing, a risk, for this slight rural girl.

I cried when I read the letter. And I later ate my peas.

When we give our kids a chance, when we allow them to experience
meaningfulness and respect, they get it.

tires

tractors red
tractors green
grandpa got run over by a John Deere
Nothing runs like a Deere

NICK
YASINSKI

Nick – 14 years old